COMING ON STRONG

COMING ON STRONG

FRANCO COLUMBU
AND GEORGE FELS

Contemporary Books, Inc.
Chicago

Library of Congress Cataloging in Publication Data

Columbu, Franco.
    Coming on strong.

    Includes index.
    1. Columbu, Franco.   2. Weight lifters—Italy—
Biography.   I. Fels, George, joint author.   II. Title.
GV460.2.C64A33   1978   796.4'1   77-23694
ISBN 0-8092-7723-9

Cover photo courtesy of Art Zeller

Published by Contemporary Books, Inc.
180 North Michigan Avenue, Chicago, Illinois 60601
Manufactured in the United States of America

Library of Congress Catalog Card Number: 77-23694
International Standard Book Number: 0-8092-7723-9 (cloth)
                                   0-8092-7565-1 (paper)

Published simultaneously in Canada by
Beaverbooks
953 Dillingham Road
Pickering, Ontario L1W 1Z7
Canada

This book is dedicated to Anita Columbu
for her endless help and patience
and
to Bud Fuller's Health Studio, Madison, Wisconsin

Contents

COMING ON STRONG

Sea Changes

Bodybuilding is by far the simplest sport in the universe, and I think that must be part of what finally drew me to it; my life, like the sport, was composed of good, healthy basics and no frills. I was born on the island of Sardinia, where processed food is unheard of and everyone works and plays hard physically. The principal export is cork, and for their living, people generally work in the cork industry or farm or do labor. Life spans are long on Sardinia, and that is no coincidence.

In Sardinian families, everyone is given his fair share of the load to pull good and early in life. My first responsibility was shepherding. The job may lack glamour, but the truth is that it's excellent for learning to be at peace with your own thoughts. I had no way of knowing it at the time, but that is absolutely the finest foundation you can lay for bodybuilding. Physique champions are some of the most contented, self-fulfilled, "together" athletes on the earth. Once you are at peace with your mind, you can do just about anything for your body that you want to.

But the shepherding and the household chores I did were generally taken for granted; after all, everybody worked, with no exceptions. I wanted attention just like any other kid does, and the best way I had to get some was to compete.

Sardinians play pretty much the same way they nourish themselves—naturally. You'll find kids who are plenty active, but you won't find many manufactured playthings designed to occupy them. They have sports, sure, but not toys and games to keep kids sitting down indoors, because they have the same net effect as processed foods. Mentally or physically, and maybe in both ways, they make you soft.

The most popular team sport in Sardinia was soccer, but in my crowd, you competed a lot earlier and more simply than that. You fought. I'm talking more about roughhousing than the kind of fighting designed to hurt anybody (although one could and frequently did lead to the next). It was mostly grappling, perhaps with an unambitious forearm blow or two, but the original purpose was nothing more than to get the other guy down and have him acknowledge defeat. And as soon as it dawned on me that people *noticed* me when I competed, I made it a point to become good at it.

I gave away size almost every time I answered the call to arms, so I was always a step or two removed from "King of the Hill," but you'd have to say that, overall, I gave as good as I got. And there was almost always one point in these encounters that I looked forward to even more than winning. It's where neither you nor the other guy is quite on your back or on your front; you're belly to belly on your sides with one hand or the other locked above in combat, pushing for an edge, trembling with exertion. I had good natural power for my size, to go with quickness, and I could usually beat the other guy to the precious leverage from there. I still remember the excited flush that comes with the tension of pushing yourself to the hilt, when your strength has done all it can and you achieve the rest of what you need with concentration and nothing else. Even before I felt the other guy yield, even before I knew he would, there was a special joy in that pure, white-heat effort and the isolated thought, "I *want* this."

My graduation from grappling and groveling in the dirt to boxing was due to two factors: television and the nagging fear that professional grappling was without future. Television was not uncommon in Sardinia, although it never captivated us the way it does Americans. We watched news and sports, little else. But one night, in my late teens, I saw a fight from Madison Square Garden featuring Duilio Loi, a world-class welterweight who eventually fought Emile Griffith and just about every other name of note in his weight class.

Loi's win that night was as much direction as I felt I would ever need. I saw myself in the ring at The Garden within the next few weeks, and without the benefits of any intermediate stages whatsoever. This is what I was born to do,

I reasoned; I will become a boxing champion instantly and fight in Madison Square Garden and make lots and lots of money—and be noticed.

I was willing to invest a few days' training before being crowned champion, so a friend and I caught the last bus to town, ten miles away, where there was a small gym for boxing training. There was a lot of frenzied activity going on, almost all seemingly having to do with fighting. The ring was busy, of course, and all over the gym, guys were belting light or heavy bags or their own shadows or skipping rope. Over in the corner, a lone athlete pumped a modest barbell into the air, and I remember thinking that certainly seemed an oddball thing to do.

We were well received. Boxing is pursued with great vigor throughout Italy, at all levels, and young talent is recruited for it all the time. In fact, the first boxing stripe you could earn on Sardinia was to make the team that went to the mainland to fight the Italian team. In a moment of generosity, I decided that I would pause to share my talent with the Sardinian team en route to The Garden and The Title, but only briefly, for I would not pass that way again. My friend and I were told we could begin training the next night, but we were hypnotized at once by the training we saw, and we stayed at the gym late enough to miss the last bus home.

Nights on Sardinia are not tropical at all, and that was one crisp ten-mile hike home. The fire in the fireplace was roaring when I got there, and the quick transition from cold to warm weighted down my eyelids in no time. But before falling asleep, right there on the living room floor, I let my mother in on my plan. And she made things even warmer for me.

"Bum!" she shrieked. (Mothers all over the world seem to have certain responses in common.) "Moron! You're going to go out and *punch* people, just so you won't have to work?"

"What work?" I protested. "Shepherding? Construction? Do you think that's the very best I can ever do?" You can hear the same dialogue recreated almost weekly on your late-night television movies, but this was better; this was Life.

"It's honest," she said, "and it doesn't hurt people." She wasn't about to talk me out of my "Title Win at the Garden," but she did have me there. So I let the argument pass and settled down to sleep.

As tired as I was, sleeping that night was no cinch. I kept seeing fists and moves and muscles, and the cheering got louder and louder. I loved my parents, and because of my lifelong concern for my well-being, I was used to doing what I was told. But here I had just argued with my mother over what I wanted to do with my life—fighting. Competition seemed the richest package that life had to offer me.

The drowsiness and the excitement flowed together deliciously, and just before falling asleep, I launched a final, triumphant, closed-eyed right cross. The punch caught my mother's best cork chair flat-footed and launched it four feet off the floor and into the roaring fire.

My parents agreed that since I seemed to be losing my mind, I should be given a chance to prove it. I could go ahead and box, provided it didn't take any time away from my job as a bricklayer. In my house, you brought your earnings home for family first, and no one was about to trade a bricklayer's wages for my lunatic dream. So I would have to work a full day, come home for dinner and household responsibilities, and *then* bicycle ten miles to town for training, since my duties would carry me well past time for the last bus. And, of course, I would have to bicycle ten miles home after training. I accepted my parents' terms in ecstasy—and to their total dismay. They didn't know how badly I could want things.

It was a Spartan regimen, but the training went well and quickly. After all, I had all the tools; anyone who could bicycle 20 miles nightly for the sake of training was already demonstrating leg power, stamina, wind, will, and a healthy hungry for high repetition exercise, which is what boxing largely is. I had quick hands and talent, too, and as soon as those facets came out, all the knowledgeable coaches and trainers in the gym swarmed to me. There were arguments over who should teach me what. I remained neutral, since that way I could absorb the maximum amount of attention. Everybody wanted a piece of me.

The bike rides home from training were a cinch. I was flushed through and through with the satisfaction of competing, and being noticed, and giving my all. The chill of Sardinian nights had no chance whatsoever against the glow I felt inside.

My performance on the job improved almost at once too. I disliked construction work with a deep passion, but now I saw it as task and reward. The work entitled me to the joy of competition, and it seemed to me that the harder I worked at my job, the more I was entitled to follow my dream.

I went through the competition in my own province like water through shampoo. The total elapsed time of my first two fights was 2:18, first-round knockouts at 0:30 and 1:48 respectively. The news quickly crackled back to my hometown on the radio. And all my relatives and my parents' friends who had put boxing on a par with joining the Black Hand suddenly began fawning all over me. Practical experience totaling 2:18, and I was a hometown hero. Isn't it amazing what winning can do?

As thrilled as I was with those victories, I felt an odd calm about them too. Remember, I had already seen all this happening before it did. Who had time to trifle with Sardinian amateurs? I had a championship to catch. *"Step aside, you,"* I remember thinking as each opponent entered the ring; *"I'm on my way to The Garden."*

Those easy wins were either the best thing that could have happened to me or the worst, depending on how you see it. With all the volumes of advice hurled at me daily, no one had managed to make the point that losing was also possible.

I continued to savage the competition in Nuoro Province. My bevy of coaches and managers said I was two wins away from making the Sardinian team; both the fighters were from neighboring provinces, and I would have to fight them there. The reports on the competition were that the first was a boxer who depended heavily on technique; the second guy was a slugger, and he was more my style. So I did a clever thing: I trained for the first fight while thinking about the second. I entered the ring in that same frame of mind, concentrating on a man I wouldn't see for weeks, if at all. And a wonderful thing happened, something that both restored my focus and made me a much wiser man.

It happened as I heard the abrupt *whap!* of my rump

meeting excellent Sardinian canvas. Those last two guys were *good,* and the first gave me special fits with his viperlike combinations and a distracting technique of stepping on my insteps, like the American fighter Willie Pep used to. He seated me discourteously for a six-count in the first round. I got off my duff and beat the guy by throwing slightly longer punches to keep my feet free, but overall I'm sure I have never been so grateful for a right cross thrown my way. I didn't enjoy it much then, but it was a brief, simple, highly memorable statement that if competition is to your taste, there will always be two items on the menu—winning and losing.

I had no business looking past that first opponent that way, and it turned out to be unnecessary anyway. I could have figured the second guy out any morning while shaving; he fought from power, exactly as I did. We showed each other a few seconds of listless footwork, mostly as a matter of professional courtesy, then came to center ring to slug for the last 2:50 of that round and the next 3:00 of the second and third. I cannot analyze how I won except to say that I simply must have wanted it more. The championship emblem he sent me home with was a black eye the size of a generous pancake. My sister screamed and scurried off to fetch me ice, two full days too late to do any good at all. But I had made the Sardinian team; the whole province already knew, and on the night of my return there was a colossal party and feast at my house. My mother bustled about all evening, making sure everyone's plate and glass were full and often looking over at me sideways and making the sign of the cross.

The next three factors that shaped my life were the summer, a poster, and a movie, in that order.

The summer brought fatigue. Sardinian summers are blazing hot, and any sane person who puts in a full day does not make much ruckus at night, much less bicycle 20 miles to train for a sport. With all my gifts for boxing, I was fighting at a mere 137 pounds; at that size, there is only so much you can ask the body to do. In a matter of weeks, I was losing both weight and strength, and the Sardinia/Italy team competition was only a few months away.

I could have slacked off on the job and conserved my

energy, but my boss's new praise for me plus my own pride ruled against that. I do not believe in backsliding in life; it seemed to me if my work slipped, so would my boxing.

"This won't work," I finally told the team coaches. "I'm falling on my face. The way I'm going, I won't last three rounds, much less win."

They were not enthused over the prospect of losing the team's newest find. "There's a way," they announced after a brief huddle. "You'll have to go somewhere else to work and train, but it'll work. You can meet the team for the matches."

"Where do I go then? Italy?"

"No, Franco. You can't expect them to train you so you can turn around and beat their brains out."

"Where then?"

"Germany. They've got some of the best training and competition in Europe."

"*Germany?* But it's almost impossible to get a visa!"

"Not now, Franco. You're a member of the Sardinian boxing team now. There are ways. People will listen. We can help you get a job as well."

It's no different anywhere else. In the Soviet Union, athletes are subsidized throughout their education and careers. In parts of Europe and Asia, full college scholarships are available to table tennis champions. Doors are always open to winners.

The first proof I saw of that was at home when I announced the plan. I expected an all-out war, but I didn't even get a mild skirmish. A factory job had been arranged that would let me send home almost as much money as I had carried home before; equally important, I had won the right to represent Sardinia. It would have been traitorous for anyone to oppose me.

A few days before I was scheduled to leave for Munich, a poster went up in the gym where I trained. Young athletes—in fact, athletes of any description—were being recruited for a novice weightlifting competition. Weightlifting has always been highly popular all over Europe.

"Let's try that," I suggested to the same friend I had entered boxing with.

"It's bad for you," he said. "I heard it makes you slow."

"In one day?"

"I don't know, Franco. That's what I heard. Why would you want to do that anyway? Isn't being one kind of champion enough?"

"Not if I could be two." I won him over. I was at peak power from the combination of hard work, sound athletic training, and eighteen years' exclusive diet of natural foods. Also, the competition was on a Saturday night; there would be no work to sap my strength.

To help us relax, we went to town early that afternoon and took refuge from the sun in the coolest part of town, the movie theater. The film was Europe's number-one attraction, which was puzzling since the lead actor was obviously not speaking his own lines. I knew something was fishy when it took him six syllables to say "Hello." The film was entitled *Hercules* and featured a spectacular American collection of muscles named Steve Reeves. He was the only part of the film that was impressive in the least.

"I could win this thing tonight with ease if I had muscles like that," I said on the way to the weightlifting competition.

"I don't know," my friend said. "I heard those guys aren't as strong as they look."

"Where do you *hear* all these old wives' tales?" I said. "The guy just tore down a whole temple!" I was somewhat naïve when it came to the ploys of filmmakers.

The strength contest was refreshingly void of rules. You simply had to get more weight overhead than anybody else. There were no clearly defined weight classes. Form or technique did not count, which was probably just as well since nobody had much of either.

I was still dwelling on Reeves. It would be some years before I was to learn the distinction between weightlifting and bodybuilding; to me, muscle was muscle. Each time my turn came, I stood motionless before the barbell, thinking, "I wonder what happened the first time Steve Reeves ever tried this." Then I slammed the thing up and home. All the competition had dropped out by the time the weight went to 90 kilos (198 pounds). I had trouble with it myself for the last 18 inches of the way; I saw myself lying in the dirt, grappling with hands locked, pushing, thinking of nothing, just wanting it.

Actually, I effected what I would later learn was a pretty fair military press. While that exercise has been discontinued in Olympic competition (as being too difficult to judge), it remains the most practical single exercise in bodybuilding, involving every single major muscle group at one point or another. I concentrated so hard that I held the bar overhead for at least five seconds instead of the required two; I didn't even hear the crowd. Every muscle in my body felt contracted and hard. I felt bigger than Steve Reeves ever was. Oh, that was a joyous five seconds. I was still thinking about it hours after I was declared the winner. My friend finished third, and I was as happy for him as he was for me. It had been a wonderful adventure, but that's all it was; I was a boxer, the future World Champion, and I had no intention of going anywhere near a barbell again.

In Germany, the emphasis in my training was to make a boxer out of the puncher. A full complement of coaches and managers worked with the last of the tools I could bring to the trade—rhythm. I didn't even know I had it, but they saw it and drew it out of me with lots of rope skipping and work on the light bag. Rhythm is the key to either exercise, and if you have the rhythm, you can master either one just by listening. Properly struck, the punching bag goes "*Sha*tata, *sha*tata, *sha*tata," and the sound is all you really need to focus on.

You can hear the jump rope the same way. People think a jump rope is something for little girls to have fun with, but actually it's great exercise. It develops stamina, muscle strength and tone, and, most important, *discipline* (you can't cheat in it). Eventually I would be having a new need for all those traits. I also learned to play table tennis in Germany, another fine game that boxers often play well because it emphasizes footwork, quickness, reflexes, hand-eye coordination, and rhythm. You learn to listen to the ball the same way you do with the bag or the rope. I play table tennis and jump rope excellently to this day, which surprises people because of the myth that bodybuilders are musclebound, clumsy, and slow. No other sport on earth is anywhere near as rich in old wives' tales as mine is, and I've heard them all by now.

There was a rhythm to my job, too, a factory production line that otherwise could have been quite dull. I locked in on

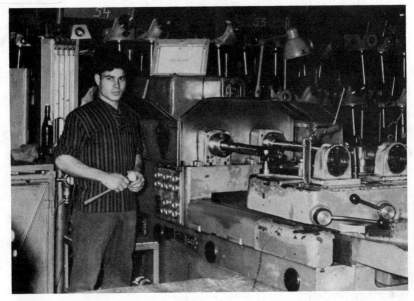

Germany by day.

the rhythm of it, and without even thinking about it much, I quickly became the best in my section at it. I didn't do it to advance; advancement was limited, and besides, boxing was where I wanted to see progress. It just seemed that as long as I was going to be in the factory all those hours, I might as well be better at it than anybody else.

By the time I joined the Sardinian team in Italy three months later, I knew that my debut at The Garden and all the rest of it were farther away than a series of half-round knockouts and cakewalks. There was work to be done. But at age 18, I had some time to spare. I saw enough improvement in myself that I decided to stay in Germany to work and train. There was no opposition from home. I had credibility now.

Weights came back into the picture in the next year, but nothing as heroic as the 90 kilos that Steve Reeves had helped inspire me to lift in Sardinia. Talk about humble beginnings: history's strongest bodybuilder began his formal weight train-

(Left) One of the best exercises on earth.
Courtesy of Art Zeller

The Sardinian team.

The left jab.

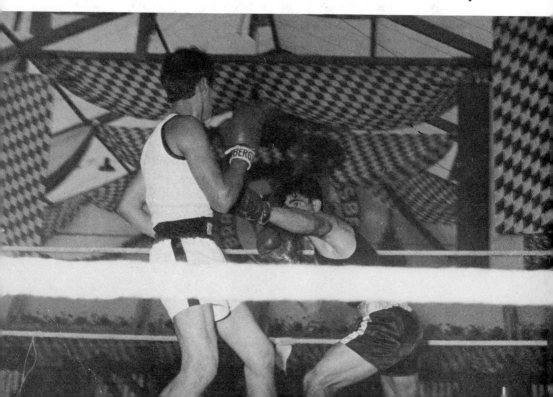

On the heavy bag.

ing with a pair of 2½-pound dumbbells. They were assigned to me for a few simple exercises designed to strengthen my punch and to build my stamina so I could carry my gloves high throughout the match. Under no circumstances was I to use weights any heavier.

They worked, too. My amateur record was 37–4–1 with 22 knockouts. In 1964, I had the choice of competing in the Italian championships or trying out for the Italian Olympic team. My handlers had begun to take my dream of turning pro seriously, but they still did not think I was quite ready for the Olympics. Their advice was to fight in the Italian championships instead. You could turn pro at once with a good show in the Olympics, they reasoned, but a poor show in the Olympic tryouts or the Olympics themselves would do no good at all. They told me to keep my momentum. If all went well, I could turn pro in the next year or so; and at the very least, I would surely be ready for the 1968 Olympics. That last notion held no appeal for me at all, but I took my disappointment to Italy and won the amateur Italian lightweight championship, as I was told to do.

But my impatience chewed up the victory joy like so much pasta. "Train for the German championships," I was told, "then the European." It was a logical plan, offered with the best of intentions, except that I did not wish to fight amateurs any more.

"I'm a champion," I argued. "Why can't I turn pro now?"

"It's not the time for it," the answer would always come back, with maddening patience. "How much money do you want, to turn pro?"

"Four thousand marks a fight."

"You'll get a tenth of that—if you're lucky." Those were smart men handling me, and they made it their business to take me to some of the fighting clubs and show me what low-end pro boxing was like. It was enough to keep me training, but the years between 1964 and 1966 weren't happy for me. I didn't know quite what to do; my dream seemed alive and stymied at the same time. I averaged a fight a month or a little more than that and never lost, but I still didn't seem to be making any progress. I drew my first taste of boredom, and few things can drive you out of a sport more quickly.

In 1966, a notice was posted in the gym announcing tryouts for the German powerlifting team. The sport, which is very popular in Europe although it's just gaining recognition in America now, consists of three events: the *bench press,* performed lying on the back, lowering the bar to chest level then raising it to arm's length; the *squat,* with the bar on your shoulders; and the *dead lift,* in which the bar is lifted from floor to waist height. I decided I would go out for the team, and my boxing handlers treated me as though I had just declared I was carrying the plague.

"You're throwing everything away!" they wailed. "It will make you clumsy and slow. Is this what we worked so hard for?"

"I didn't work this hard to fight amateurs, either," I replied, knowing all. "Besides, it's something to do."

My boxing credentials didn't impress the powerlifting coaches at all. I still weighed only 137, and there was nothing showing that predicted a great powerlifting future for me—not yet.

The German powerlifting team.

"Do you have any experience at this?" they asked, acting more bored than I would have liked.

"Of course," I snapped, bending the truth politely. "I was the Sardinian champion." And they sat up and took notice.

I made the team more through my talent for pestering people than through raw brawn. I wanted it badly enough, and between a lot of desire and modest talent, I hung on to make the trip to Stuttgart. We were taken to the gymnasium where the matches would be held, and there were so many athletes on the floor working with weights it seemed that no organized competition could ever get under way.

"All these guys are powerlifters too?" I asked a teammate.

"No, some are bodybuilders. There's a physique competition first. We have to wait."

"What happens then?" I asked, having had more than my fill of waiting.

"Nothing much. They don't lift weights or anything on-stage. They just come out and pose to show their muscles, and whoever's built the best wins."

"Who decides who wins?"

Winning. That's Arnold, topless, behind me.

"Judges."

"And that's a *sport?*" I said. "That's what we're waiting for? What a waste of time! I could tell them that now, if that's all they're waiting to find out. The tall guy there is in a class by himself. Now why don't they get their silly business over with so we can lift?"

Despite my recommendations, they went ahead and judged the thing formally anyway, eventually picking the same winner I had. The Junior Mr. Europe of 1966 crowned that night was 17-year-old Arnold Schwarzenegger of Austria. It was his first victory ever.

As for me, I concluded my competition, as horse racing

followers say, with the field in view—dead last, out of 19 entrants. I showed little humility over my finish but rather a
good, healthy flair for melodrama. "I'll be back," I announced, to snickers and giggles, "and I'll beàt all you guys."
I did, too, and soon. I went from last in the German powerlifting championships to first in the *European* championships
in six months' time, while my boxing career continued unde-
feated and going nowhere at the same time, and my coaches
looked on aghast.

I worked my tail off improving my powerlifting in those
six months, as you might suppose. Naturally, the time for that

had to be borrowed from boxing. My boxing routine had peaked anyway. I saw nothing to be added to it, and therefore it had become less something to look forward to than something to have done with. I just didn't feel that my training was helping me grow as a fighter at all, or maybe it was just my frustration at not being able to turn pro. But it had been nearly three years, and boredom was setting in. How clear it is in hindsight that my boxing career was finished for all practical purposes right then.

Before long, Arnold Schwarzenegger appeared in my gym, looking for more weight to handle and a better atmosphere to handle it in. Soon after that, he had a job as an instructor there.

"I saw you lift in Stuttgart," he told me one night.

"Why would you remember me?" I said. "I was terrible. I smelled up the place."

"That's why I remember you," he said. "I thought, 'Why would he be here when he's out of his depth like that?' And I decided it must have been because you wanted it badly enough."

"Yes," I said, amazed at how well he seemed to know me already, "I did."

"You've improved since."

"I certainly hope so," I replied. "I'm working my ass off."

"Listen," he said, "why don't you schedule your training so we can work out together? These other guys are shit. I need some competition, someone who can handle the same kind of weight I can. I need to run faster."

"Why?" I said. "Where are you going?"

"To the top."

That was my kind of talk. "I see," I said. We began training together right after that. We both increased power tremendously as a result, but not because of clever training. What we did together initially made very little bodybuilding sense. We just tried to beat one another in each of the powerlifting events. If we got into a bodybuilding regimen at all, it was largely to screw up one another's muscles for the next test of strength. Arnold was pretty hungry for wins, even then, and he would encourage me through a brutal routine for the arms, then challenge me to bench-press. You're lucky if you can bench-press your body weight once your arms are fully pumped. But I guess I must have wanted the wins too, because I fell for it just about every time. Sometimes I even beat him, despite all his shenanigans. I was holding my own against him in the strength contests in no time, when he deigned to make them fair.

I was not anxious to plunge into bodybuilding just then; I was more interested in raw power. And bodybuilding reminded me of Olympic weightlifting; it was a specialty, having little to do with real strength. Olympic weightlifters are strong in the press, the snatch, and the clean and jerk. But those events are performed standing straight up, and that is not the body's most powerful position at all. The powerlifting events are performed in the body's real power modes, supine and crouched, and are therefore a better test of the lifter's true strength. And the one bodybuilding contest I had seen seemed to me to be another of strength's by-products, nothing more. One advantage I would ultimately hold over the rest of the bodybuilding world was that I crossed over to the sport from power training first.

"With all that power," I asked Arnold once, "why are you so concerned with just standing around flexing your muscles?"

"Because that is what I have decided to be the best in the world at."

"I see," I said.

"Does that sound foolish?"

"Not to me." My German was only fair at the time, but the man obviously spoke my language. It was hard not to like Arnold. He knew just what he was doing and where he was going, two qualities I envied because of my dissatisfaction with my future prospects in boxing. And whatever was said to him, he seemed to have fun with.

"How long will it take you to catch Steve Reeves?" I joked, finishing a punishing set of arm exercises.

"No time at all," Arnold answered cheerfully. "Reeves is shit. I can beat Reeves right now. I will beat everybody in the world shortly."

"Then I suppose it's you I should aim my sights at," I said, disappointed that he had so little to say for the man who had inspired me once.

"Yes," Arnold agreed, "you might as well aim as high as you can. You can always get it if you want it enough." Then, seeing that my arms were good and tired, he challenged me to arm wrestle, a strength test of epic dumbness, and beat me— barely.

The next morning, I could barely move. Undiscovered muscles the length of my arms were singing to me, and in arias this Italian artisan had never heard. What's more, they were singing most shrilly, no more than a half-tone apart.

I did manage to dial the phone. "You idiot, Arnold!" I hollered without saying hello. "I'm in *agony!*"

"That's because you did everything correctly," he said merrily. "It's working. No pain, no gain. You're on your way, Franco."

"I'm on my way to the madhouse, and you belong with me," I said. "I should have known you were a little off, Arnold. The guys in the gym are shit, Reeves is shit, the whole world is your privy. And shit is what I feel like this morning, too. Goodbye." I could hear him whooping happily as I hung up. It was three days before I could train for anything again. But in those three days, the initial soreness went away, and what was left was a warm, drowsy, not unpleasant sensation in the muscles; and I felt sorry for unloading on Arnold that way. I thought of bodybuilding then as a possible change of pace from my powerlifting routine; that was all I wanted from it then.

But within a few weeks, I wanted even less from boxing. I scored my 22nd and final knockout in a match, and my poor opponent went to a hospital, where he would stay for two months. In 21 previous knockouts, I had seen people wave ammonia under the fighter's nose and help him to his corner and then to the dressing room. This time the ammonia didn't rouse the fighter, and I'll never forget how the brief joy of winning came crashing down on my chest when I saw him just lying there. I visited him often in the hospital and con- tributed what I could toward his bill.

My managers tried to make the point that he would be all right, that it was all part of the game. But I was horrified at what my hands had done. I had thought only of winning, not hurting people.

I took my unhappiness out on the weights. It's not an attitude I'd recommend to anyone else for weight training because it's negative, and nothing can undercut your training like negativity. But I was mourning the loss of over three years' investment in a sweet championship dream, a loss that needed replacing.

Last place in a German competition is a peculiar foundation on which to build a new dream of world conquest, but that was all I had. I was not interested in being a laborer all my life, not in Sardinia or Germany or anywhere else. That thought alone was enough to keep me going.

Because I was looking so hard for things to love about powerlifting, I found them. The patient process of building the bar to suit you, over and over. The way the muscles feel locked into place when the bar is at its lowest. The way the floor seems to groan "Thank you" when a successful dead lift is launched, and the flush of pride that comes in that exercise in the final triumphant straight-back position. The way the pectorals flatten to form a landing strip for the bar in the bench press, then arch to blow it a kiss goodbye. And finally, the excitement of the added strength you can feel almost on a daily basis that makes up so many times over for the slow-moving, one-repetition-at-a-time training. You can feel it in the body's most powerful muscle groups, the thighs and lumbar regions, right where it feels the best, and it seems like you will never be vulnerable to injury or harm again.

I branched out into some of Arnold's bodybuilding exercises too, sometimes with him, sometimes not. They felt good to me now, and after three years of trainers and managers and sparring partners the aloneness of the business felt good too. If the boxer couldn't grow, at least the body could. In the boxing gyms, I started to hear a lot about how good I was starting to look, and I thrived on that. I liked the way I looked and I wanted to stay that way; that was all I asked of bodybuilding then. And in the weightlifting gyms, I saw powerlifters I knew looking at me sideways, as though they were hearing my footsteps coming up on them; I thrived on that too.

Boxing training went all downhill after that. In my next—and last—fight, I pulled my punches for nine rounds, afraid to connect and hurt somebody else. My handlers told me we couldn't win the fight without winning the tenth round big, and that woke me up enough to make me get to work and win the thing—barely—on points. The love affair with boxing was over, and I was ready for another championship quest on the rebound.

That is how I got started, and it proved to be the perfect start. I had will, discipline, rhythm, and power, plus peacefulness about myself. Arnold has often said that if he could have had my gifts for his own beginning, he would have been even greater at his peak.

I've seen guys enter the sport for all kinds of reasons. Men pick up barbells after breaking off with their girls, not too dissimilar to what happened with me and boxing. Some come to iron just in pursuit of physical fitness, a strategy I cannot wholly endorse. And, yes, men often enter bodybuilding for remedial reasons, just as in the old Charles Atlas comic book ads. They are some of the best-motivated athletes in training, too.

But the bodybuilders who do best in my sport generally fall into three categories. There are the athletes who train specifically for the contest level. They are a tiny minority; out of the more than 20 million who train with weights in some way, there are only a thousand or so bodybuilders in the United States who are qualified to compete above statewide level. And I would suspect that very few of those came to bodybuilding with the contest level in mind; they mostly just liked what they were doing and decided to go ahead and take it as far as they could. That's what I did, and I don't know of any other sport that so easily gives you that choice.

Then there are athletes who train with weights to improve their performance in other sports. There are more of them than you think, especially in the pro ranks—and they're not just football players. Bodybuilding complements any other sport on earth quite well. The exercises can be as specialized as one wishes to make them, and they build power and endurance whether the athlete is actively interested in an increase in size or not. So those who choose bodybuilding as a second sport enjoy increased benefits in both.

But in many ways, the bodybuilders who are the most successful of all are those in the intermediate or advanced intermediate stages. These are men who recognize how mental the sport really is, and therefore it becomes a hobby. They recognize the joy of pushing oneself to the hilt and, more selfishly, seeing their gains, not to mention feeling the incredible body sensation we call "the pump." You should see the expression on the face of a man who realizes for the first time that he is easily handling more weight than he did his last time out. The sheer joy of seeing your body advance from any single phase to the next is worth the pain ten times over. The reward for this group of bodybuilders is a build that is striking without being abnormal. (I think it's fair to call contest bodybuilders that—much fairer than to use some of the other words we hear.) Again, the sport becomes unique; nowhere else will you find intermediate practitioners who are as confident and proud of their accomplishments.

As powerlifting was still my first sport then, I continued to meld the training disciplines of powerlifting and bodybuilding, and I still do. Not many bodybuilders do that, and it's an important distinction. There is some truth in the notion that bodybuilders are often less strong than they look, and that is a function of improper training. Those builds do not last as long as muscles that are correctly trained for power as well as size. For example, you get a joker who notes that the biceps and pectorals are the easiest muscles to pump. Now those are attractive muscles to look at, but almost nonfunctional to one's strength; the sole function of the biceps, for instance, is to bend the elbow, and there are just not that many elbow-bending applications in life requiring giant power or size. So our man proceeds to pump biceps and "pecs," with no thought given to strength *or* proportion, and winds up looking like he's smuggling four cantaloupes. That is not what my sport is about.

When this misdirected athlete—and he's not unusual in

Competing.

bodybuilding—finally does recognize how silly he looks, he will very likely quit. Since his "muscles" are really just bloated tissue, they'll disappear in a short time (but they won't turn to fat, as popularly believed.) Nature will take back the improvements you attempt to make on her, unless you go about it correctly.

My first improvements showed up in the eminently correct places, the power zones. One normally sees his first bodybuilding improvements in about six weeks, but I threw myself into a frenzy of training. The rhythm of the routines came to me just as it had on my job, and I had began to grow as though in time-lapse photography. In less than three weeks, I could see a crevice down the middle of my lower back, thick fingerlike ridges of definition molding my shoulders, and giant teardrops on the insides of my thighs. Then my chest began to bloom too, and I was on my way.

And the *pump*—oh, my friends, how good it felt and how

greedy for it I was. Training a muscle with weight actually tears down muscle tissue; but each time, proper rest and nutrition then rebuild it slightly stronger than before. Thus the athlete grows and becomes stronger. And Nature gives you a head start on nutrition by pumping extra blood to that torn tissue, tightening the muscles under the skin until the skin feels ready to burst, and making the exercised muscle measurably larger for hours. The harder you work, the more tissue you break down; hence, the greater your pump. The blood charges up there and you can feel it seem to surge and swell like November seas.

Of course, like many bodybuilders, I began carrying my elbows wider than my shoulders almost at once, as though my back had already begun to flare. That is a sort of apprentice card among iron-pumpers, and most of them begin affecting it before Nature has actually given them reason to. I have always seen a gentle irony in the fact that some of these guys then turn around and denounce the posing phase of physique competition.

I probably jumped the gun a little myself on elbows-out, but the real thing wasn't long in coming. As with most sports, first improvements are often your fondest; there is a special magic in the First of anything. And I remember the time I stood before a mirror, actually saw for the first time the sea changes taking place in me, and thought, "No one can stop me but me, and this is really going to work." That evening I probably carried my elbows slightly under shoulder level.

My early months were the peak of my immodesty about my build. To be candid, I found ever-increasing occasions to take my shirt off. I had heard the boxing gym humming with words of how good I looked, and I could never hear too much of that. I particularly enjoyed swaggering around Munich's swimming halls, even though I've never especially favored swimming. I had a lot to learn about the way my sport should be properly represented, but I've remained totally unopposed to being noticed. Once again, I had a future world championship to announce.

If you want to teach a kid to play football or basketball or almost anything else, the first thing he wants to do is scrimmage and the last thing he wants to do is drill or train. Bodybuilding is just the opposite: millions will happily train, but only a few wish to compete.

The sport frequently does attract football players on a part-time basis, and one of the memorable clichés of that sport that I have heard is this: you never know how fast your receiver can really, really run until you throw the pass a little bit farther in front of him than usual; if he wants it badly enough, he'll get there. What I had thrown in front of me was one of Europe's great physiques in the form of my training partner, and I ran like hell to catch up with Arnold and his head start of two or three years' training. That was another exclusive advantage I had as a beginner; yet another was that I was building from trimness. The world's finest bodybuilders prepare for competition by first adding weights and decreasing repetitions to gain bulk, then doing just the opposite to define, or "cut up," their size. Only I and a handful of others believe in trimming first and building second; that way there is never any excess to be dealt with. Besides, that is how I got my start, and there are times when it is wise to stick to what you already know.

I gained on Arnold admirably, although that was largely because I had farther to go, and probably also because, at that point, I had no designs on competition and therefore was not trying *too* hard. But I was hungry enough that we were good for each other in training. He corrected my mistakes and helped me see how limitless the training really is, once you understand your true potential. "Come on, Franco, lazy bastard," he would say just as I could feel muscles beginning to scream. "I want two more repetitions at least, two if nothing else." And I would give him those two repetitions and more, thereby giving him footsteps to listen for and making *him* run harder too. We stayed longer and later in the gyms and used more weight more ways than anybody else. Everyone thought we were both quite mad.

But I think that if you want to excel, at whatever it is you do, you must first make up your mind that you will appear different from the others. If you looked and did the same as everyone else, how is it that you would excel? The kids in an average sandlot football game don't look like O. J. Simpson either, but the next one who does will surely appear very different from all the rest.

Very early in training, I discovered that my muscles and I were talking to one another. "That's enough," I could hear them say as the weight lowered to the last critical few inches or repetitions, and I would say silently, "No, not quite," and they would say, "All right, then." And we'd see it through together. Between workouts, even lying in bed, I could feel that surging growth that I wanted so badly, and hear the muscles saying, "We know. We're coming." It was just a by-product of having spent so much of my early time alone with my thoughts, but the communication served my training well.

Both the sport and the training itself are more mental than I can ever tell you. You are literally what you think you are; the best of us constantly see and feel ourselves to be just a smidgen bigger than we might really be, and thus the striving never stops. That's why you see a guy strutting around elbows-out half an hour into his very first workout. That is how he sees himself, realistic or not; if he stays with it, that is what will happen too. It's quite magical.

The mental pleasure of watching a muscle grow is at least the equivalent of the physical pleasure of the pump. The nature of all living things from the amoeba on up is to grow; Nature will do everything she can to help you if she sees you mean business. That's how my dialogues with my muscles came about; and while competitive bodybuilders have never been polled on this, you may be sure they're all talkers too, admitted or otherwise. We treat our muscles like living things, which is to say with respect.

This dialogue with muscles is how most of us learn to pose; as long as you're going to address the things, you might as well get a good look at them too. Strangers to the sport usually find something affected about the posing phase, but it's just an athlete checking his progress in a mirror—as golfers and tennis players often do—and it's a real art and science in itself. Many effective poses are based on ancient Greek sculpture and the later work of my countrymen during the Renaissance. We don't know for certain, but this is pretty fair evidence that our sport has really been around in some form for centuries.

Posing is as versatile as training is. There are some poses to highlight size, some to show muscle definition and separation—even some to show striations, another of Nature's gifts to me because of my head start on power in training. You learn most of the poses not for competitive purposes, but as progress checks, and also as a useful adjunct to training. Poses are nothing more than isometric drills, and tensing and squeezing the muscles that way during a workout helps the pumps.

In shifting over to competitive posing, you add a *few* moves that do not normally figure in daily training, but not too many. Posing for competition is very much like Olympic figure skating; there is a base of some compulsory moves, followed by the athlete's optional routine. Correctly done, this will be a smoothly flowing sequence from one position to the next, each a demonstration of symmetry plus whatever other feature or features the athlete wishes to display. Poorly done, of course, it's just embarrassing.

When I decided I would give the Mr. Italy contest in Verona a try, as a one-time adventure similar to the Sardinian lifting meet I had won once, I put together a posing routine based on the rhythm that had worked so well for me in boxing. Most bodybuilders strike a pose and hold it heroically; I thought it might be memorable to pop off a series of more and quicker moves, just like skipping rope or working on the bag. So I worked on speed and my sense of what looked best for me. Good posers always add a few points to their scores, sometimes even enough for a victory margin over a slightly better body. I've always prided myself on being one of the better posers, and one of the very few to put together a speed routine that way.

My work was cut out for me, however; there was a combination of hometown favorite and hometown judge whose reputation as a team was known as far away as Germany. In every team sport, the home field is supposed to offer an advantage, and that is true now and then in bodybuilding too. It shouldn't be, but it is, and this was an advanced case—so much so that, weeks before the actual contest, everybody expected the local athlete, Franco Fassi, to win and his brother, Virgilio, to finish second.

(Left) Roots. *Courtesy of Dr. Anita Columbu*

By the time an audience sees a physique competition, the results are largely already in, from the *pre*-judging phase that takes place that afternoon. I frankly thought that I had the Fassis dead to rights, but that alone would not be enough to sway Judge Ruggiero Tampellini. I simply would have to look as good as I could for the pre-judging and then win the crowd over to help me put together a victory. After all, I was Italian already, and that gave me a big edge on any other visitor.

A contest customarily begins when the curtain is opened on the full lineup of contestants. What the Veronans saw first, that evening of my first contest, were 40-odd contestants in posing trunks and one odd Sardinian, 'way the hell off to the left, in a red satin robe. Just like Sylvester Stallone in *Rocky*.

I wasn't all dumb. Whom do you suppose everybody looked at first? And when I heard the place buzzing over who or what that might be, I slipped out of the robe and hit a pose. Everybody else was standing naturally, but there's no rule that says you have to. My move stampeded the field into a flurry of unprepared, awkward poses. Some of them bumped into each other. By the time they had all assembled their poses, I was standing naturally, grinning at the crowd.

Franco Fassi was taller than I was, so he competed in a different class; the best of the talls (5'9" and over) is a finalist against the best of the shorts (under 5'9"). I went to the finals of the Short Men's Division, where a pose-off was called between Virgilio Fassi and me. I thought I was going to win and posed like it. He had been worrying about me ever since he had seen the satin robe, and he posed like a beached whale. No contest. Even Tampellini couldn't save Virgilio Fassi.

Franco Fassi was another matter. He beat a very good field in the talls. While I had excellent proportion, my size was unspectacular; Frano had an edge on me in chest and arms. But by the time we were called for the last pose-off of the evening, I was the crowd favorite and, for added momentum, a better poser too. The crowd began to chant in cadence to my rat-a-tat poses: "*Fran*-co Co-*lum*-bu! *Fran*-co Co-*lum*-bu!" leaving no doubt as to the Franco of their choice. I had never heard cheering like that, not even for all my knockouts, and I hoped the gooseflesh would not detract from my poses.

The pose-off went on much longer than it should, and on

The endless posedown.
*Courtesy of Universum
Sportverlag GMBH*

Note how bushed Franco Fassi looks.
Courtesy of Universum Sportverlag GMBH

Mr. Italy.
Courtesy of Universum Sportverlag GMBH.

my frontal poses I could see Tampellini poring furiously over his charts, trying to find a way to take this away from me. We posed on and on; Fassi grew tired and so did the audience. My boxing conditioning was an added edge. I had so many poses to begin with that I could simply start all over again and no one would remember. And I did. I must have run through my full 30-pose sequence four times.

The fatigued crowd had quieted down. After all, it had been nearly 20 minutes. So you could hear it all over the auditorium when Fassi turned to me and said pleasantly, "I'm very tired."

"I'm not," I said.

"I'm going to quit."

"I'm going to stay."

"You should," Fassi said. "You're the best. By far." Tampellini looked up with a puzzled frown and a stern *"Silenzio!"* for the two athletes, still posing, conversing calmly as though at class reunion.

"What's taking so long?" I asked.

"Tampellini," Fassi called out to me. "I really don't know

what he wants from me. You're built better anyway, and I'm about to fall on my ass. Even if I win this, I'm going to say that you should win."

"Thank you very much," I said, and the crowd now modified its chant to one for the head of Ruggero Tampellini. He concluded his 20-plus minutes of meticulous score taking by throwing 20 sheets of paper up over his head. He stormed up to me onstage, raised my hand, and said with a furious scowl, "You win."

If there were more than 40 contestants in the Mr. Italy contest of 1967, at least 30 of them were nice enough to come up to me and suggest I go ahead with competition. Here I had a national championship less than a year after I had begun training, and bigger contests were looming with wonderful names like Mr. Europe and Mr. World and Mr. Universe.

My ability to absorb praise was as limitless then as it had been when I heard all the oohs and aahs over my first improvements in the boxing gyms. I knew after the first three compliments that I was now going to train for two world championships instead of just one; but I still managed to accept the next 27 expressions of kudos with innocence and grace.

I called Arnold when I got back to Germany. "How did it go?" he asked. "Did you win anything?"

"Just first is all," I said. "I expect to beat everybody shortly."

"Well," he said, "maybe not *everybody*."

"We'll see," I said. "You and I are going to train together, and improve together, and before long we're going to compete together. And we'll see. Meet me at the gym tonight."

"I'm training in the afternoon today. I have a date tonight. Make it tomorrow."

"Then I'll start tonight without you," I snapped. "'Tomorrow' is shit."

2

Moments of Truth

I gave bodybuilding a lot bigger chunk of my life right after I won that first title, pursuing bodybuilding and powerlifting at the same time six days a week. Before long, I replaced my factory job with an instructor's job in a gym, and that is when iron became my passion.

You'd think my new job would have made infinite training available to me, but the case was just the opposite. I had to be ready for instruction, help, and questions all day. That's when I learned the value of forcing the pace of training, achieving maximum exercise with minimum rest. To this day, I don't know a top competitive bodybuilder who trains as fast as I do. They're in the gym when I get there; they're in the gym when I leave. Two hours is all I ever train (once in a great while, two two-hour sessions a day). I believe that is the limit to how long you can ask your body to give its all. I can't understand it: I train the way I pose, bap-bap-bap, from one thing to the next; and all the competition put in their plodding four to six hours daily and shake their heads and call me lazy. "Lazy," my ass. Two hours is enough time to lift 60 tons.

So I was able to feel and see growth and change almost daily. When an athlete does enter this phase of weight training, and it can happen long before he's even remotely ready to compete, he makes giant strides in self-awareness too. A simple yawn and stretch becomes a luxury, almost an indulgence. Just as the bodybuilder flushes up muscle from within, he gets into himself from the outside, and this two-way process is a textbook lesson in getting to know oneself. Bodybuilders are frequently introverts, although Arnold is a notable exception.

The one discipline in my sport that did give me some

trouble was learning not to favor any muscle group. I wanted to do more of the exercises that felt best to me, naturally, and so do most bodybuilders in existence. But you don't *dare* do that, because proportion is what wins my game, and you can't overtrain certain muscle groups at the expense of others. A basketball player may decide whether he likes to shoot or pass or rebound best; football is also specialized in many ways. But the bodybuilder has to do everything or he can't play the game.

Along with the Cantaloupe Smugglers, there is another strange bodybuilding species we call the Light Bulbs. These are the guys with terrific upper bodies who teeter about on stork-thin legs. That's just laziness. I'll grant that calves are tough and somewhat boring to train, but they're worth a try. All over the world, calves are bodybuilding's stepchildren.

I naturally favored the powerlifting muscle groups, the shoulders, back, and legs, and my chest training actually got off to a slower start as a result. Most bodybuilders thrive on chest and arm work, but you know by now that I am not like most bodybuilders. Chest and arm muscles are well padded when relaxed, but the back and shoulders and thighs are always hard. And I loved the way they tensed as the bar descended, my hardness against the iron's—and mine always won. I thought of those muscles as my private stable of fighters. No wonder I was so fond of them.

Better bodybuilders started coming around to my gym, once the word got out that the instructor was Mr. Italy, and I've found that this sort of thing happens all over the world. In my sport, as in many others, you can learn from other athletes whether they are as advanced as you or not, and part of what makes the best bodybuilders so good is that they are always hungry to learn. Arnold's gym and mine were the most popular in Munich in no time.

So I had a chance to see more bodybuilders and more kinds of training than ever, as I worked toward the Mr. Europe and Mr. Universe contests, two and four months away, respectively. To this day, I can tell more than you'd think about a man by watching him work out. The sport is self-starting by nature, so that says something right away about athletes who train seriously. A man who works hard at exercises but has them in incorrect sequence (and sequence is very important) is almost certain to be taking a long, disorganized way around something else in life. If a guy fails to put the full exercise motion to work, or "cheats," it's a safe bet he takes the easy way out somewhere else, too. The bodybuilder who spends most of his time just looking at himself between sets probably just goes through the motions in other things too.

But those are not good bodybuilders, and I was seeing lots of good ones, who created a competitive atmosphere that was invaluable for me. And good bodybuilders make the clearest kind of statement about themselves and their discipline. If you were working out and had completed an exercise to the point of pain and exhaustion, and somebody walked up and offered you a million dollars to grind out a few more repetitions, you'd do them somehow, wouldn't you? Serious bodybuilders reach back and do them for themselves alone. Their breaths become grunts and groans and finally shouts, but they get it done, and everybody cheers everybody else on. You wind up pulling like hell for a guy who could well be your next competitor—but you might as well. You can't stop him anyway, and if your heart is in this, his best will only serve to make you better too.

With a national title to my credit, the gym saw that I was attracting others to the place and let me set aside two hours daily for uninterrupted training. That was a big help, but I also had to gain weight. I had not yet begun a competitive bodybuilder's diet of four to five meals a day, and I had a 24-inch waistline when I began, so I gained weight slowly, three to four pounds between contests. But it was exactly the right kind of weight, slabs and slabs of muscle, and at my size, that kind of weight gain showed up easily. My waistline grew to 28 inches without a gram of fat anyplace, an unmistakable sign of correct power training.

The Mr. Europe contest, two months later in Brussels, was actually easier than the Mr. Italy contest. For one thing, the judging was eminently fair; for another, as I would learn once and for all upon coming to America, European bodybuilders are just not all that good. They train basically for symmetry, which is correct, but they don't seem motivated to pursue real depth and clarity of muscle, the finished look. The

Mr. Europe, 1969. *Courtesy of Universum Sportverlag GMBH*

field had symmetry; I had symmetry plus hardness, and I leapfrogged past everybody. I deserved to win and I did.

Two months later, in the Mr. Universe contest in London, the sport dealt me a lesson of sorts in humility. You still can't convince me I should have lost, but I did, winning my class but finishing second overall to an Englishman named Wilfred Sylvester. It was a stunning accomplishment for someone who had been training less than two years, but it left me anything but satisfied. Sylvester was built just as I described, nicely symmetrical but not wildly muscular. Of the handful of bodybuilders who *ever* beat me, he was easily the least distinguished, and I made a true spectacle of myself demanding to know why I had lost. Only once in my life would I ever lose anything less graciously than that.

It's very difficult for bodybuilders to get their actual scores, or any contest details at all, for that matter. Normally they will tell you who wins the top places, and nothing else; if you learn anything more than that, it's usually through politics or just some judge's looking the other way and being nice. Neither was the case in London; I raised such a stink that they talked to me just to quiet me down. What they told me strongly suggested that either I or they were losing some marbles.

"You're too muscular to be a Mr. Universe," they explained.

"And that's an *answer?*" I screamed. "How can you possibly be too muscular to win? Isn't that the *idea?* What the hell is this, a beauty contest?"

"Well, yes, that's the idea. But then again, no."

"Could you take me through that again?" I said.

"A Mr. Universe champion represents the male universe. We want him admired by other men. If it's someone as muscular as you, they can't relate."

"If I was that worried about what the average guy thinks," I said, "I wouldn't have worked my heart out trying so hard not to be average."

"Oh, you have a wonderful build, Franco," the officials said. "It's just that you're too muscular." And the logic eluded me again.

Later on, I would be able to see some misguided truth in what they said. As I've said, European contests do generally place symmetry above all else; that is exactly the way Steve Reeves was built, and that is why he became such a remarkable box office star all over Europe. But what also worked against me, probably at least as much as the emphasis on symmetry, was competing against an Englishman in London. The combination of native son and/or unqualified judges does in many a better body all over the world, fully one contest in four. If the pre-judging or judging starts to take any time, it's a sign of nothing good.

I resolved that I would never put a contestant through anything like that. In my career I have been a judge many, many times, both in contests I've produced and in those produced by others, and it's never taken me more than a few minutes per athlete. If you know what you're looking for and how to look for it, that's all it takes.

What kept me from getting discouraged at that point was my continued success in the power events. I had been the European middleweight powerlifting champion for four years in a row, increasing both my totals and the distance between me and the field annually till world records fell. Muscularity accrues naturally during that kind of training, and eventually I could see that being screwed out of a Mr. Universe title after less than two years' work did have a negative promise in it. I did not expect to be penalized the world over for being too muscular.

Did I work! Sometimes I went to Arnold's gym to train, and sometimes he came to mine, but in either case I had some of Germany's best bodybuilders and one of Europe's best to set a pace of sorts for me. And I outran them all.

I underwent attitude changes, too. Like all advanced bodybuilders, I dropped the elbows-out strut as kid stuff and began to represent my sport with dignity. Bodybuilders who want to make the sport look good, as it has done for them, save their posing for the contest stage and carry themselves as proud, good athletes, which they are. You'll see in them the kind of posture that every man should have; show me a good bodybuilder with poor posture and I'll show you a genuine idiot. Perfect posture comes naturally to us. But strutting does

Posing in Germany.
Courtesy of Benno Dahmen

(Opposite and above) Posing in Germany.
Courtesy of George Greenwood

not, once the sport has made us mature (which it does unfailingly), and you won't see much of it.

And attitude carries us well past a way of walking. My German was quite good by then, naturally, but bodybuilders seem to have a bond that needs no language. The sport is such a highly mental thing that the men who have successfully challenged their barriers of pain and exertion already have a special sort of communication. Bodybuilders are extremely communal. As complete strangers, they will nod hello on the street when they can recognize someone who shares the sport. They will go out of their way to help each other in training, whether buddies or strangers. They will answer a beginner's questions and offer advice with endless patience, as long as they think he is sincere. You might get snubbed now and then, but I think in that case you would have encountered both an oaf and a fool. I'm proud to say my sport knows damn few of those.

More important than all of that, bodybuilders have a decided flair for understanding their fellow man. When you learn to treat your body with respect, you learn to do the same for other people.

Ever since my shepherding days, I had had a zest for privacy that carried over into training to some extent, and I still have. But you can't weight-train in a vacuum. For one thing, exercises such as the bench press and squat carry some risk unless you have a second athlete standing by to help in case you have trouble with the bar. We call that spotting, and to ask a total stranger to spot you is perfectly within the sport's decorum. And further, bodybuilders are nice people to· know. They have a great degree of acceptance of who they are, a quality that is hardly common to all men.

I was using so much weight for the power exercises that I usually needed two spotters. I could hear them grunting a duet of admiration, and even though your concentration is meant to go into the exercise and nowhere else, that always spurred me on. There's a certain sense of mind-over-matter mastery that comes with the assembling of hundreds and hundreds of pounds for oneself to use, and that kept me pumped up mentally as well.

The legs have the most amazing muscles by far. They are

insanely strong to begin with; a man in generally good health
can lift 150 percent to 200 percent of his body weight with his
legs with no trouble (there's even a special apparatus for pre-
cisely that). And my legs had the added advantage of more
than three years' boxing training. So I was ready. But even I
was surprised at what I could do.

Many hundreds of pounds were a necessity for me in all
the powerlifting exercises, of course. The dead lift was my
best single event for sheer weight handled, but I think I enjoyed the feel of the squat even more. It's rather like life itself;
you don't really find out what you're made of till you're down
as far as you can go.

Correct breathing had my rib cage expanded by the time
I got down there, and I could feel my ribs braced against my
thighs, matching hardnesses. And even though that was my
point of peak vulnerability in the exercise, that was when I
felt the strongest, everything locked into place, all the power
in my back and legs billowing like all the air in my lungs.
"Goodbye now," chest would say cheerily to thighs; "see you
next time down." Then I'd explode into erectness as though
the iron had insulted me personally by even suggesting that it
might win. And I couldn't wait to get back down there again.
That's when you really find out about yourself, just a few
seconds at a time—but how it all adds up.

Then I'd go on to the leg exercises for shape and second-
ary muscles, movements that make the legs "burn" the way
your forearm does after sawing wood, and facing up to that is
a completely different kind of discipline. And finally, the stubborn calves, which you win over more by persistence than by
science. There is only one calf exercise of much value, rising
up and down on the balls of the feet, and it's to be done with
as much weight for as many sets of as many repetitions as the
athlete can perform. It's a simple but tough muscle, the calf, a
real bitch to pump; but mine talked to me reassuringly. "All
right," I'd hear, sometime during the sixth set (20 repetitions
each) or thereabouts, with the weight of two men on my
shoulders, "we'll get there; be patient." And I'd reward them
with two more sets, plus a few more repetitions, pigeon-toed
for maximum pressure on the muscle. You ask the muscle to
do all you know it can, then you do more. The bodybuilders

The calves. *Courtesy of Art Zeller*

who get the most out of that "more" phase are the ones who go farthest. Now substitute competitive spirit for sheer muscle and you have the makings of a champion in the sport of your choice. Real winners can go full tilt and still always have something in reserve they can reach back for.

And I had all that fun with the least fun part of the overall routine. Upper body work is lots more satisfying, which is why you find so many intermediates doing little or nothing else. This is the phase of training that helps a bodybuilder perceive his muscles as "deep" instead of merely "big"; and as you think, so do you become. Most of us do chest and back exercises on the same day, a technique that also works the shoulders from two directions at once. The bodybuilder who successfully accomplishes a chest pump and back pump on the same day leaves the gym feeling impregnable to just about any

Benching.

force on earth. Upper body training makes you feel that deep and that good.

The best single chest exercise is the bench press, rather like a pushup in reverse in that you lie on your back and push the weight away from you. I hold the world record at this in my weight class, with a lift of 485 pounds, and I frankly think it will be a long time coming before that record falls to any other middleweight powerlifter. But that achievement was not the product of pure power; there's another secret that I mastered early.

As the bar is lowered to meet the chest, the pectoral muscles flatten; they are not used to being compressed that way, and there's minor pain involved. It's not the kind you'd confuse with the real pain of injury, and the bodybuilder quickly learns to tell one kind of pain from the next. But it's uncomfortable enough to make you think, and as the muscles tire with repetitions, the pain grows. No pain, no gain. It's nothing more than up-front dues paid for post-training pleasure, task and reward all over again. Still, the pain plus that awesome descending bar brings a fear along with it, and the two grow together.

The bodybuilder who wins out over the bench press—and goes on to test the true limits of his strength—simply learns to trust his power rather than fear the pain. And that's far more a test of concentration than brute strength. The pain is both-ersome but tolerable; the trick is to *think* it out of your chest and into your head where it can be dealt with. The body-builder who sets his mind to "I can take it" is well on the way to winning and need hardly dwell on anything else. Because then the girders of strength that connect the shoulders through the chest respond and take over, boasting "There's power enough here, hell, yes; power enough and plenty more besides," and all of a sudden there's the bar back up there at arm's length again.

I got the knack early, and a love for the exercise along with it. I wouldn't have been nearly as good at it otherwise. But that's what I had to do to isolate maximum strength for maximum benefit. You commonly see guys lowering the bar less than all the way, or arching their backs, or surrendering the bar to their spotters in the middle of their last repetition, and they think that they just weren't strong enough. That's not it, because they don't know what their strength really is. It wasn't the weight that made them quit; it was minor pain and major fear. Once you break away and get yourself free of that, you can add upper torso strength in layers.

Arnold and I also led the league in taking the sun and skipping workouts. Germany is not known for its sun, nor is there any reason for it to be; but we made the most of it. Contest stage lights can wash out definition and details and highlights that were months in the making; if two physiques are perfectly matched, the better skin tone will win. All those Italians I defeated in my first contest had all that sunning opportunity, and they all still had the color of uncooked pasta—even the Fassi brothers. I never forgot that.

As for the missed workouts, we were simply less stubborn

about those than the rest. When we trained, we trained the hardest; but when we just didn't feel like it, we knew there was no way to benefit from it. Others would train come hell or high water, forcing themselves through the sheerest kind of drudgery. Even if they don't know the difference, their bodies do. The muscles say, "If you're not going to get into this, why should we?" and the bodybuilder ends up exhausted, sometimes over-trained or even injured, but almost always without benefit. Heads wagged and tongues clucked whenever Arnold and I missed a day, but we knew what we were doing. We trained when we meant business, which was most of the time; we skipped when we didn't, and that kept our viewpoint fresh. No one has ever just plain enjoyed training the way Arnold and I did, and I'm convinced to this day that that was a major factor in our becoming the two best of all time.

Arnold and I never did go head to head until 1972, which was several years after we had both come to America. Before that time, we were not competing in the same level of contests. So the only real competition between us was the friendliest kind, within the gym. We helped each other train for our respective contests. We hosted and promoted contests of our own, too. I even invited that silly Tampellini from Verona to come to Germany and be a judge for one of my shows. After all, he'd done me no real harm; and away from home where he had no reason to see anyone special win, he was a sound, qualified judge, and those are hard to find. He accepted my invitation and judged flawlessly.

The regimens for those who train just to train and those who train for contests are worlds apart: the posing, for one thing. Contest bodybuilders spend hours and hours before the mirror, and not because of self-love or anything like that. Mostly they concentrate on the six or seven mandatory positions, which are the same all over the world, looking for the same proportions the judges will. The spread of the upper back muscles (specifically, the *latissimus dorsi*) from the front, to display width, V-shape, and proportion between back and chest. A side view of the chest, showing muscle thickness and proportion to arm and waist. A double biceps pose, rear view, demonstrating arms, upper back, and balance to rear leg mus-

The crab.
Courtesy of Caruso

cles; all but the very best lose points here. Another latissimus spread, from the rear, this time to check the back's proportion to waist and legs. The *other* side view of the chest, to make sure the athlete does not have a "good side," which occurs with bodies just as it does with faces. Then the double biceps from the front, showing arm size and depth. And finally, the "Most Muscular" or "Crab," in which the athlete contracts every major muscle group at once. It's an impressive pose, but the trick is to do it with a relaxed face. Not many can do that, and the grimace that often comes with the pose makes it look like a last-resort remedy for constipation.

In 1968, Arnold defended his title in the European version of Mr. Universe; he is still the youngest ever to win that. He was contacted then by Joe Weider of California, the most important single name in the sport and the head of a body-building empire that sells three million magazines a year, not to mention equipment, weight-gain supplements, and other products. Weider offered Arnold an expenses-paid entry to the International Federation of Body Builders' (IFBB) version of Mr. Universe in Florida, and the prestige of the event was too much for Arnold to resist. He went and was narrowly beaten by an American named Frank Zane, who has been part of bodybuilding's very top circle for close to a decade today. The defeat disappointed Arnold greatly, and Weider, with charac-teristic good timing, told him he could beat anybody in the world if he would only come to California and train for a year.

I had my doubts. In the first place, I did not truly believe that California even existed. In Italy, when we are upset, we tell one another to go to California the way Americans tell one another to go to hell; we simply don't think one ever gets there. Secondly, I did not want to see my best friend one continent away.

"How can it possibly be any different there?" I persisted. "Do they know anything you don't? Does the weight weigh more there?"

"No."

"Why go then?"

"Franco," Arnold said, "I don't like losing. Not at all. There's very little I wouldn't do, if I thought it meant I'd never lose again."

My first three contests were enough to establish me as one of the best bodies in Europe. Actually, my having roared through the ranks like that made me something of a sensa-tion, and I had my own loyal following from that point on. But I think my love affair with audiences began even earlier.

I had competed before responsive, emotional crowds be-fore, of course, in boxing. But let me tell you, it's not the same sound. All the years I spent listening to little besides the mutterings of sheep made my ears highly tuned and sensitive, and I could tell the difference. Someone has to get hurt before a boxing crowd will respond, and so you can always hear a few jeers for the guy you have decked mixed in with the cheers for you. You don't notice the jeers at first, because the first few times you feel only the thrill of people cheering for you; there just isn't anything else in the universe that can enter your head at that moment. But after a few times, you can hear the edge of that second sound too, and it's actually unpleasant. It's somewhat cruel and ugly to hear, and the sound doesn't seem pure any more.

That's where bodybuilding is different. There is no one to fake out, knock a ball away from, or hurt; there is only you, and so the cheers are pure again. That was the sound I wanted in my ears, ever since the crowd had virtually insisted that I win at Verona. No sports crowd on earth makes *quite* the same sound a bodybuilding audience does. They are close-knit, for one thing, like the athletes themselves, and they are fiercely loyal to the sport. Some of the cheers seem to be agreements with the muscles popping to life: "*Yes!* That's *it! Def*initely!" You see many of the same faces at different meets, even when the meets are in different countries. They will encourage new talent like the boosters of few other sports I know of; they will be courteous, even responsive, to lesser athletes in the sport too—except in those unhappy cases in which someone shows up who has no business doing so. Bodybuilding audiences cannot accept that; that is not taking the sport seriously or respectfully, and they will make the athlete squirm before he's done.

But when they're on your side, they cheer you so beautifully. Their love for the sport is almost on a par with yours, and you can just about hear the love flowing in the cheers: *"Thank you for representing this beautiful sport so well."*

We all spend a good part of our lives looking for people to cheer us in one form or another—one we can marry, others we can work for, and so on. But when people actually leave their seats and *cheer* you—really, really cheer you that wonderful way—and you're standing there feeling the combined pumps of a backstage workout and your posing contractions, enjoying the competition, and having an awareness of being one of the strongest, best-developed bodies in the world—it would seem that there is little else to ask of life. Anyway, not for a former shepherd who wanted to be noticed.

I have a mild temperament, which is probably just as well. My fighting skills plus my power make a totally lethal combination, even today. I've had my share of rows—there always seemed to be some dunce who just had to challenge my build—and while I always make it a point to give better than I get, I do not dare hit a man full force.

But I can be pushed beyond my limit, too. In 1969, I was working in Regensburg, Germany, 60 miles from Munich, as an instructor in a gym. One night I was replacing the weights at closing time, nine o'clock or so, a point in my working day I especially liked because I had devised a little quick-repetition routine I could go through with the various barbells and dumbbells as I put them where they belonged. That night somebody went and spoiled all my fun.

One of the women instructors came into the men's gym and told me that two drunken imbeciles were making a fuss in the reception area. They wanted to play table tennis, which we had available; they wanted beer, which we did not have; and they wanted the two instructresses as well, which was out of the question.

I wasn't happy to hear this news. I was enjoying my little put-away routine plus the lift that comes to most people at the end of the working day; and besides, I don't like bullies. Say what you will about bodybuilders; you will find very few bullies in our midst. It's beneath us.

By the time I got to the reception area, things were worse. The other instructress was backing away from one visitor's sudsy advances, and the gym owner, a pleasant man in his 60s, was sorrowfully tending a bloody nose. Our guests' breaths and bellies announced Germany's finest malts and hops, and I knew at once what I wanted with cretins who threaten women and punch old men.

"The gym is closed," I announced with all possible patience. "I earnestly suggest you two assholes leave at once."

They moved on me immediately, proving their pea-headedness. Although they couldn't know about my boxing

Courtesy of Dr. Anita Columbu

background, I had won the Mr. World title, a fact that did show; and there was no reason for any rational man to single me out for combat. I dispatched the two clowns in tandem, one or two punches each, dragged them out, stacked them neatly, and sat on them to wait for the police.

Six weeks later I received a registered letter from a Munich hospital, with a bill enclosed in behalf of two patients admitted there with exotic jaw fractures. The combined charges were 5,500 marks—$1,650 or thereabouts, and every bit of five times the money I had or could raise.

The courts regard debt differently in Germany from the way they do in America. In America a lawyer can stall for you till Judgment Day. In Germany a semiofficial institution like a hospital can get an injunction against you; if you don't pay, you can go to jail.

But my first complaint was against the logic of it, not the finances. Here two idiots had come looking for trouble, found what they were looking for, and now I had to pay for it? I went to the gym owner and told him it was his turn to defend me. He contacted his attorney, and the best deal they could get for me involved my paying the bill and then suing for recovery in the courts. That didn't help me at all; I still didn't have the money, and I wasn't about to borrow more than two months' pay from the gym to pay anybody's hospital bill. I had one choice left: leave the country.

I contacted Arnold, who had been in Los Angeles for about a year under his contract with Joe Weider. He worked out something hurriedly for me, a contract that paid very little money but that had an added incentive plan if I could win the IFBB Mr. Universe. Bargaining power is often a function of time on your side, and I had neither.

To get a visa to America, you must show the consulate a round-trip ticket to prove your intention to return. That left me with chillingly little pocket money with which to change worlds. You must have a smallpox vaccination, too, and at that point in my life I had not been inoculated against anything. When I was in school in Sardinia and the time came for shots, I would always run away in a dazzling burst of ignorance.

So the smallpox shot really laid me low. I boarded that

plane looking as though I were drunk. It was a rocky flight, too, with rain the last few hours. We landed at Kennedy Airport, which on a rainy night in June is about as comfortable as landing in the middle of a rubber plantation; and I was sick to begin with. I had hardly any money, and absolutely no English. The customs officer managed to get it through to me that I would have to continue to LaGuardia Airport to get to California. The notion of two airports in a single city bewildered me in my fog, but somewhere in there I had heard the name of another Italian, and that was a balm of sorts.

I landed in California weak, pale, and underweight. I was probably in the worst physical shape of my life. Arnold and Weider were good enough to meet me at the airport, and they nearly missed me; they were looking for a bodybuilder. I showed Weider my diminishing biceps in place of more formal identification.

It wasn't the most dignified way to arrive in America. Both in the way we spell our names and in the way we came across, you'd have to say I fall a little short of Columbus.

3

America

By coming to America, I started to find out what real body-building is all about. There was a whole new world of competition as well as a whole new world outside that, and I entered both as something of a mute. I had the languages of still another world, and only Arnold spoke either of those.

Still, as I said before, bodybuilders everywhere have a way of communicating that doesn't need words. I learned English mostly in the gym, of course; in my first months in America, that's where I had almost all my contact with others. And I'm convinced that speeded up my learning the fundamentals of the language. When you know something of what's in a man's head and heart, his words come to you easily.

I was very happy to be in California, too, and in that frame of mind one can learn anything quickly. The warm sun reminded me of my days as a boy in Sardinia; the typical Southern California drivers reminded me of my days as a Formula III racing driver in Germany, a field I had entered briefly. I felt right at home.

At the same time, how I felt the differences. Every country I had ever been in seemed at least 100 years behind America, and even now that bodybuilding has sent me all over the world, I still feel that way. Many of the things Americans have long since taken for granted left my jaw hanging. Flying from Rome to Munich and back, for instance, means traveling 700 miles each way, paying about $300, and returning on a flight that is available once every two days. In America, to travel the same distance—between Los Angeles and San Francisco—one pays only about $45 and leaves on the hour of one's choice. It took me a year to get a passport in Europe;

Making our own kind of music.
Courtesy of Art Zeller

You can't keep a good man down.

With Tom Bradley, mayor of Los Angeles.

in America you take two snapshots to the post office and complete everything in three days. An Italian driver's license requires 20 tough hours of study, a thankless test, and a stiff annual tax; as evidence of the ease with which one acquires a driver's license in America, I need only point you in the direction of Santa Monica. I got my California telephone in one day, though I had spent six months getting one for my parents' house in Sardinia. Can you imagine how these things appealed to me, with my zest for compressing time?

The differences in the people are even more striking. In Europe, Germans hate Italians and Italians are pissed at Austrians and Greeks thirst for the blood of Turks, with all kinds of vice versas. It's hard to express what it feels like when you see somebody actually smile upon hearing that. you're from a foreign country. Americans are truly interested in you and your plans and your goals; they want to help if they can.

Most of all, I was overwhelmed by the opportunity here. It's very much like bodybuilding itself: if you want to grow badly enough, you've got a highly promising shot at it. If you want to be a professional man in Europe, you can generally forget about it unless you are the son of one. I came to America with no money or mastery of the language, just some strength, and in seven years I became both a world champion in my sport *and* a doctor. There's just no arguing this: there are two reasons, plain and simple, that Arnold and I are the two most successful bodybuilders of all time. One is that we both entered the sport with a foundation of abnormal power. The other is that we both came from Europe, recognized the whopping opportunity America offered by contrast, and exploited the situation. (That we enjoyed it the most didn't hurt either.) Having been on both sides of the fence makes you considerably more expert on the greenness of the grass.

These aren't naïve views. I know there are always whiners and complainers; and without dissent, America would not have been born at all. But all I can say is, if you see a flaw in the American way, wait till you see the options.

Every bodybuilding contest I personally produce begins with the National Anthem, as every American sporting event should. I encourage the audience to sing with the recording; I like it that way. You don't *have* to sing, of course, but don't let me find you sitting down.

The competition in America took some getting used to. In Europe, my best bench press was 420, and that entitled me to lord it over just about everybody, including many of the heavyweights. But the sport actually varies from country to country. In Italy, they train mostly for definition; no one gets very big, but their "cuts" are phenomenal. In Germany, it's just the opposite—lots of size but not much definition (maybe it's the beer). In England, of course, the emphasis is on symmetry. Only in America do the athletes really put everything together. Over here, guys bench-press 400 as though it were some kind of lark—even athletes for whom weight training is merely an adjunct to some other sport. I was a Mr. World when I came here, yet I was dwarfed by middle-of-the-pack bodybuilders. It was unreal. My first few weeks in California, I often caught myself grinning like a fool, openly admiring what American bodybuilders can accomplish.

Then I went to work, and I improved my bench press to

485, where it is today. I've heard of marathon runners' referring to the last six miles of their event as "The Wall," and I don't doubt that's what the experience is like. But those last 65 pounds of my bench press felt like a damn mountain. That improvement was nearly six years in the making.

So the atmosphere in America certainly made me run faster, and I suppose you'd have to say Joe Weider did too. Articles on or by me have appeared in one or another of his magazines just about every month since I came to America, along with dozens and dozens of testimonials and endorsements. You can still run across me in the back pages of *Esquire* if you look carefully enough. I wasn't able to read any of the articles at first, naturally, but that wasn't really necessary. For anyone as aware of a following as I was, the glow had already begun.

I didn't just work harder; I learned too, picking and choosing tidbits and chunks of others' routines as though the gym were a Chinese restaurant. No two men are ever built exactly the same, not even identical twins, and so it is unlikely that the same program will be ideal for any two men. The percentage of men who *never* put their optimum training routine together is high, terribly high. And what's rarest of all is the athlete who is totally satisfied with his routine. You get stale, just as in anything else, and you *have* to change or your attitude suffers. Each time you reach this stage, the experimenting begins all over again.

The differences among the best bodybuilders' routines may be very minor, but they are there. In all the years Weider has been publishing various athletes' routines in his magazines, I'll bet you won't find half a dozen complete duplications. It's all a matter of trial and error; some exercises may be so wrong for you that they actually retard your progress. And while exercises that *feel* the best to you are generally in fact the best ones for you, you can't count on that. You must wait and see, as long as two to six weeks, to observe the results of any significant change in routine. Needless to say, I was not good at the game's waiting phase.

The time it took me to put together the ideal routine cost me a few contests. I had begun to add the size I needed to become world class, but I would not reach my peak for

Before.
Courtesy of Art Zeller

After.

Courtesy of Art Zeller

Before.
Courtesy of Art Zeller

After.
Courtesy of Art Zeller

Before.

Courtesy of Art Zeller

After.
Courtesy of Caruso

Before.
Courtesy of Dr. Anita Columbu

After.
Courtesy of Art Zeller

another 20 pounds. I lost to Frank Zane in the 1969 Mr. World, but I have beaten him three times since. And in 1970, I lost one version of the Mr. Universe contest to an athlete named Chris Dickerson. I quickly passed him, too, after that, but I think Dickerson's win was good for the sport. He had the attention of the media to some degree; he was discovered working as an usher at NBC and had made some appearances with Johnny Carson. So bodybuilding got some good publicity for a change, and that's worth losing a contest for, at least to me. That year, however, I did win the IFBB Mr. Universe.

That's when I began to make money out of bodybuilding, something I found just about as addictive as the sport. Not only was Weider paying me more and sending me all over for paid exhibitions, but I had enough confidence in my English to begin my series of training pamphlets, one for each of the various muscle groups. So my mail-order business began, and it still flourishes today.

The first time Arnold and I were booked into Germany, we were guest posers for the Mr. Munich contest, and that's where we encountered "the Screamer" that Arnold talked about in the film *Pumping Iron*. Arnold's version of that story is doctored somewhat to feature himself more; you have to remember that Arnold is not bashful about the limelight to begin with. But I was there in Munich, and I was part of that story too.

We asked for an early morning workout so we could get something done. What generally happens is that we get more attention than we want when training on the road. We get ogled, in fact, and it becomes rather uncomfortable for us (for me, anyway) because we're accustomed to working out alongside other champions who are used to us and who mind their own business. So we try to avoid crowds in unfamiliar gyms.

But the Screamer was already there that morning, a real jerk and a bodybuilding species we had dealt with before, the type who inflates his ego without bothering to pump up his muscles first. He recognized us right away and advised us that he expected to win the Mr. Munich contest. Heaven knows why. He had the shape and color of contoured bedsheets, and the only curves interrupting the smooth blobs of whiteness were not muscles but blotches and pimples. Not everybody can be built the way we are, naturally, and we wouldn't put the man down for that alone. What rankled us was his over-blown view of himself and his underrating of our sport; the idea to screw him up occurred to Arnold and me at once.

We politely asked him to pose, and he posed like an idiot, including some we had never seen before, some sitting and even some lying down. Totally worthless, of course. He must have thought the function of posing was simply to see how many positions one could achieve. It is not; the function of posing is to display muscle, of which he had none. Even if he had had any, it would have been obscured by his mindless poses.

"Now. What tips can you give me to help me win the contest?" he demanded.

"You might want to try chess," I muttered, but he didn't hear me.

"I think what you ought to do is scream with each pose," Arnold told him. "That's what judges are looking for today—macho."

"Yes," I agreed, "and with each pose, you want to get closer and closer to the judges so that you and they are as one for your climax." If Arnold could keep a straight face through this, so could I.

He agreed at once, and Arnold and I went to work on our discovery. Arnold handled the audio aspects of the performance, I the visual. Arnold taught that the pitch of the scream must be dictated by arm position; I blocked out sweeping strides downstage between poses, like an operatic diva, my Italian heritage contributing nicely here. The night of the show, Arnold and I watched from the wings to see what we had wrought, and the Screamer didn't let us down.

"*Nnnnnnnngggghhhhhh!*" he mooed, from a flat-supine position. I swear I saw five judges straighten in their seats immediately.

"*Hoooooooooo!*"

"*Aaaaarrrghhhh!*"

Each of these was punctuated with single dramatic strides downstage, per my teachings. Bellow and stride, bellow and stride, pose after awful pose. After 30 or 40 seconds, the audience was moved to respond and began roaring back at him. Arnold and I held each other up to keep from falling down laughing.

And they didn't drag him off the stage, either; Arnold just likes to tell it that way. The Screamer got his full two minutes onstage. *"Yeeeeeeeaaahhhhhh! Uhhhhhhhh! Gahhhhhhhhh!"* The show's promoter, an extremely conservative man named Rolf Putziger, was way at the back of the auditorium, but even in the wings we could hear him pleading: "Get that maniac off the stage! He's ruining my show!" But there was too much noise for anyone to pay much attention. The tubby specter advanced on the judges until he was just about ready to lurch into the orchestra pit, "hanging ten," as California surfers say. Then he squatted politely and screamed in the terrified judges' faces.

The reason Arnold tells this story differently is probably so that he'll come out on top. Remember what I said about European enthusiasm for bodybuilding? The Screamer got an ovation that Arnold or I would have been proud of.

And at that, he insisted furiously that we tell him why he hadn't won the Mr. Munich, especially with his new ploys. We told him the judges weren't sophisticated enough for him.

Sometime in 1970 I flew to New York for a contest and met Mike Katz, a bodybuilder with an oversized chest and heart enough to fill it.

Mike was literally goaded into being the biggest and strongest in his circle, by so-called friends who called him names like "Four-Eyes" and "Fatty" and "Jewboy." These friends were clearly smaller than Mike to begin with, but he went ahead and made himself over well enough to become both a Mr. America and a professional football player. Today he is one of our sport's very best examples of brains and agility, two qualities bodybuilders are not always given credit for. He's an assistant principal in the Connecticut school system, and he has played pro ball for both the Jets and the Raiders.

The thing about Mike is, he wanted to become big so badly that he became too big. If you heard Ken Waller, another ex-football player and schoolteacher, analyze Mike's build in *Pumping Iron,* that analysis is correct. That chest and back are so huge that it is impossible to bring his other muscle groups, the legs and arms, into proper proportion. Mike can balance a glass of water on his chest when it's fully pumped, but that stunt will not win him any contests. He's been trying to win the Mr. Universe for four or five years now; I hope I'm wrong, but I don't think he will. Training his waist and his calves causes him problems, and at 245 pounds, those problems show.

I'd like to see him win a U, and so would just about everybody else. Nothing is too much to ask Mike Katz to do for you. The first time I met Mike, he took me with him to his home and family in Connecticut, fed me, put me up, trained with me, squired me around, offered me his car to use on my own, and more—all before we even really knew each other.

Of course, the same things that cause him to be so friendly and so appreciative of good friends make him incredibly sensitive too. And because of the mental nature of bodybuilding, his sensitivity can actually get in the way of his progress. The first time he came out to California to train for a contest, he asked me what I thought of his build, and I told him, "You look a little smooth, Mike." In bodybuilding jargon, that means some work is needed on muscle definition; it's not a word the athletes welcome. "Don't worry about it. We'll do some high-repetition work and some running, and we'll burn that off."

He thanked me for the good advice and immediately sought out a second opinion. This time he ran into Dr. Mike Walczak, a physician who takes bodybuilding seriously and who minces no words.

"You look fat, Mike," he told him.

"But Franco said I only looked a little smooth."

"Franco's still learning English. The word is *fat,* Mike. You look fat."

Mike Katz came to me in deepest sadness. "Dr. Walczak said I look fat."

"Get to the gym and get to work," I told him, "and stop worrying about what people say."

Part of the reason he came to California in the first place was to train with me, but in his new zeal he began going to the gym alone. Gold's Gym, where we all trained then, is in Venice, a community that Southern California is not terribly proud of. Mike asked the manager there for still more advice.

"Venice is full of hippies and creeps," Mike said, "and I can't always come here with Franco. Do you think it's safe at night?"

"You're *afraid?*" the manager asked. "Mike, who's gonna mess with *you?* You're as big as a monster. You look like Frankenstein!"

That failed to bolster Mike's spirits.

"That's not what he meant, Mike," I tried. "He didn't mean that you look like Frankenstein; he meant that's how *big* you look. Frankenstein was a big guy."

"Yeah," Mike Katz said. "Sure."

"He was, Mike. Eight feet. More."

"I'm not ugly?"

"Of course not. Just big, that's all."

"Big and fat," he moaned, and he spread himself across my sofa, so depressed that he fell asleep almost instantly. He was so huge that his head hung over the edge of the sofa, and sleeping that way, he looked as though he had beheaded himself for his flaws.

A day or two later, Mike, Arnold, and I and a few others were taking the sun after a workout, and Arnold saw two black girls who appealed to him. He told us he was going to try for some numbers ("Phone number want" were the first three words he taught me in English), and he did engage one of them in a brief but lively chat. Then he came back.

"How'd you do?" Mike asked him.

I wish you could have heard Arnold's Austrian accent trying to capture her black dialect, because it defies spelling. "She said," Arnold reported cheerfully, "'Hey, man, how come you talk like Dracula?'" He didn't seem fazed in the least, laughing right along with everyone else.

I suppose I should have let it go, but Arnold had been bringing out the competitiveness in me for three or four years by then. I wanted a laugh too, and I just couldn't resist. "It's not many guys," I pointed out, "who get to take the sun with Dracula and Frankenstein at the same time."

"Or individually, for that matter," said Arnold, who was

no help at all. I could see that Mike Katz was slipping toward coma. It took an extra half-hour of cajoling to undo what I had done with my big mouth, and that left me more exhausted than barbells ever could have.

Mike had a chance to write articles for the Weider magazines when he trained in California, too. Most prominent bodybuilders love to do that. It's a treat for their followings, and besides it pays—about $150. Also, it's a chance to share knowledge of the sport, something we all enjoy doing.

So, armed with a tape recorder, Arnold and I took him up into the Santa Monica Mountains to help him compose his article as we took the sun. We also had some wine.

I drove. At the time I had a beat-up old Volkswagen, and I took us up the tough, skinny mountain roads in a manner worthy of an ex-Formula III professional driver. It made Mike Katz very nervous. At one point I could hear him murmuring: "Too fast. So fast. Oh, so fast. Slow him down. Please. I don't want to die. I want to live. I want to pose."

Both the sun and the wine were warm and delightful. Arnold enjoys the pleasures of the grape as well as the next fellow; as for me, I am Italian. After the three of us were well drenched, we hauled out the tape recorder and fashioned Mike's article in interview form. Some of our questions dealt directly with training; others touched on fringe areas such as fidelity, frequency, and potency. The topics were staggered quite nicely, as I recall—one question on training, one on sex. At the conclusion, the compleat works of Katz were nicely steeped in nasty secrets and even included the author's recommended contest diet of wine and spaghetti.

The article and our sunning finished, Mike blundered into a modest error in judgment. "Arnold," he said, "would *you* drive? Franco makes me a little nervous."

"Of course," Arnold said grandly, "I don't drive a bit like Franco."

I decided I would trust Arnold's instinct for survival, which is considerable, and go along with this plan. Still, this was the *downhill* run, a double threat when coupled with Arnold's nonchalance about such niceties as blind curves and double yellow lines. The views on the way down were wonder-

With Arnold and Mike Katz.

ful, and Arnold showed us just as much view as we could possibly see and still survive. I don't think he touched the brake once on the way down. Mike Katz is half Jewish, and he called upon each God in turn—many times, too—to just bail him out of this one and he'd never ask again. Arnold whooped and bellowed happily all the way down. I laughed to the point of tears myself, once I was sure that we were in fact going to live.

We dropped off Mike's tape with Joe Weider the next morning. Our excuse for not sticking around to listen to it with him was that we had to go and train. I never heard anything about it again; neither Arnold nor I dared ask. My guess is that we set back Mike Katz's entry into journalism quite some time.

1970 Mr. Universe, Belgrade.
Courtesy of Benno Dahmen

I think the finest overall field I have seen in any single
contest (exclusive of the Olympia, which consists of a handful
of Universe winners) was the 1970 IFBB Mr. Universe contest
I won in Belgrade. I had won my class in the 1969 version of
the U, which was sponsored by both the IFBB and the American Federation of Amateur Bodybuilders (AFAB), and now I
wanted it all.

The heavyweight class was especially impressive, with
Sergei Nubret from France, Chuck Sipes and Mike Katz from
America, and lots of other 240-pounders from all over Europe
and Asia. I thought I looked like the runt of the litter, and I
was nervous enough to visit the men's room every hour
around the clock without fail. But I beat them all. This was
the first government-sponsored Mr. Universe contest ever, and

1970 Mr. Universe in center.
Courtesy of Benno Dahmen

therefore the first to be internationally recognized. After my win, I was taken to the government palace, where I met every official there was to meet except Tito himself.

That got me good and pumped mentally to defend my title in Paris in 1971. I was ready to win physically as well. The Universe, remember, is actually a team event. Countries send teams comprised of entrants in each of three classes. France and Arabia had bumper crops of athletes that year, and so did some other countries, but overall the field had been stronger a year earlier, and I had won then. I was a clear favorite this time.

So I was disqualified.

I don't have the slightest doubt that the one thing led directly to the other. Contest officials came to me no more than a minute or two before I was to pose. I thought they were joking at first.

"You cannot pose, Franco."

"What are you talking about? I pose as well as anybody here."

"That's not what we mean. You *may* not pose. You've been disqualified."

I waited five seconds, then said, "What?"

They waited forever, studying their shoes, then repeated themselves.

"Why?"

"There've been two protests. Mr. Universe is an amateur contest. They say you're professional."

"Professional?"

"That you posed for equipment ads." I was beginning to catch on. Dozens of guys do that, including plenty who were in that same contest. But there was only one favorite—me.

"Who made the protests?" I asked.

"France. And Arabia."

Of course—one less American to beat, one more medal they could win, more points for their country's team. I looked around furiously. Not a French or Arab athlete in sight, naturally. It would have taken someone with a true death wish to fool with me then.

I moved toward the contest stage.

"Franco, please," they pleaded, "you can't blame us."

"Who, then?"

I parted the curtains and stepped onstage unannounced. There was a great roar, which changed in tone the instant I passed the posing platform. My intentions were clear seconds later. I vaulted the orchestra pit, landing in front of the judges' table, and that table ceased to be. I know only a few rudiments of karate, but I somehow tore that table to bits with my bare hands. Water pitchers, glasses, scoring sheets— all went sailing out over eight rows of the audience.

When order was restored, the judges got even with me through my teammates. No American won his class that year. I seethed for hours, and somewhere between madness and rationality, it occurred to me that there was only one foolproof way to be safe from that kind of shit. I would have to become not only the best, but the best ever.

I never lost again, except to Arnold. And today, six years later, you can find followers of mine who will tell you that I made that dream of being the best ever come true, too. That is open to debate, which doesn't hurt my feelings one bit. Whether I ever actually achieved that goal or not, I made one hell of a run at it, and that will have to do.

The two all-time best, Arnold and I
(opposite and next four pages). *Courtesy of Art Zeller*

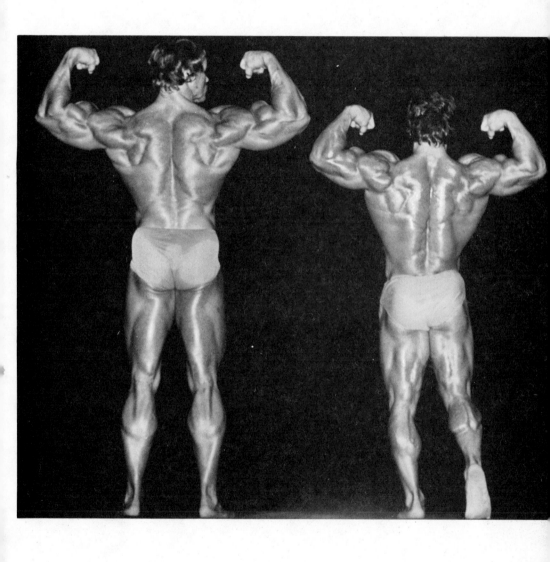

4

Beneath the Surface

Some of the damnedest questions are asked about body-builders, and the answer to most of those questions is "It varies," especially those questions dealing with smartness, agility, and certain physical endowments.

Sooner or later, the drug question comes up. It follows the sport around like some kind of mugger, waiting to drag us down at the first sign things are getting good for us.

It's not without truth. I can think of very few body-builders, including all the sport's big names, who haven't at least tried anabolic steroids. So have shot-putters, wrestlers, and other athletes to whom physical bulk is worthwhile. But the drugs' use as a matter of general habit is widely overrated.

I once tried Dynabol during a precontest blitz, which is when most bodybuilders get around to the drugs. They are good for a quick spurt of weight gain, five pounds or so, but very little else. Many authorities will tell you that the weight gain is mostly a placebo effect; whether the athlete endorses that theory or not, there's no arguing that the true effects of the drugs will not be felt for at least two weeks, all negative effects into the bargain, including permanent, irreversible damage to liver, kidneys, even the family jewels.

Bodybuilders will wolf down vast quantities of vitamins and protein supplements, and I guess you'd have to say those are "drugs," all right, but they're hardly what everybody thinks of when they hear bodybuilders use drugs. I personally think those things are of limited value in gaining weight and therefore as overrated as the steroids are. What happens is that the athlete's system will simply say, "Very interesting, but we aren't going to assimilate all this for you. Better hit the

Courtesy of Art Zeller

Courtesy of Stuart Sobel

men's room." Weight must be gained gradually, for body-builders as for everyone else. The body tends to seek out the weight it's used to; for exactly this reason, people who have dieted successfully will bounce right back up in weight unless they're very careful.

As to bodybuilders' smartness, I'd say the range is mostly from bright to very bright. Bodybuilders are better educated than is generally thought; the discipline of one is excellent for the other. Three of the biggest names in the sport today—Mike Katz, Frank Zane, Ken Waller—are teaching or have taught school, and there are lots of other examples of bright bodybuilders.

The charge that bodybuilders are "muscle-headed" comes up now and then, but that is so much foolishness, as are the notions that all bodybuilders are muscle-bound (very few are), that they're all gay (very few are), that all the muscle will turn to fat (impossible), and so on.

But as to muscle-headedness, let me point you instead in the direction of the men who *run* bodybuilding. There are some exceptions, notably Joe Weider, whom I respect as a businessman because of his respect for a profit. *Muscle Builder* and *Muscle Power* magazines, Joe Weider Health and Fitness, Body Persuasion System, Inc., Weider Communications, the Weider "Method" of bodybuilding, Weider Protein supplements, Weider Tanning Oils, Weider lifting belts, apparatus for curling exercises and for crushing exercises, and entire home gyms—Weider, Weider, Weider.

Contrary to what people may think, Joe does *not* make money out of competitive bodybuilding. Just the opposite, in fact; he makes his profits from advertising his products and services to the millions who train *without* competing. The athletes associated with him are the best in the world, which reflects credit on Joe, to be sure. But Joe's support of contest bodybuilders is basically generosity; it is certainly nothing he needs to do.

No Weider publication is complete without the work of my good friend Art Zeller, the finest bodybuilder photographer in the world. Just as there are experts specializing in photography of food, fashion, cosmetics, and so on, so it is

With Joe Weider. *Courtesy of Art Zeller*

with bodybuilding; very few know how to do it the right way, and none knows how better than Art. He is a keen student of the sport; he knows all the stars and what makes them that way, is as well qualified as most contest judges, and never fails to capture the subtle features and highlights that vary from one athlete to the next.

Joe Weider and his brother Ben founded the IFBB in the late 1940s. Eighty-seven countries are members now, and it's the 11th-largest sports federation in the world. This was a

direct challenge to Bob Hoffman, president of the York Barbell Company of Pennsylvania, chairman of the AAU (Amateur Athletic Union) weightlifting committee, and Olympic
weightlifting team coach for years and years. Hoffman pub-
lishes a magazine, too, called *Strength and Health*. His magazine heavily favors weightlifting and its athletes over bodybuilding and bodybuilders, but Hoffman is not about to walk
away from bodybuilding completely, especially now that it's
on the rise. The Weiders and Hoffman (and later, Dan Lurie
of Brooklyn) have been bickering and feuding forever.

Sometimes individual sponsors cannot get their own
houses in order, even when there is no conflict from the others. In 1974, for instance, I was appointed to choose the team
for the IFBB Mr. Universe, along with Tom Minichiello, a
true bodybuilding expert who owns one of the finest gyms on
the East Coast. We chose Ken Waller, Robin Robinson, and
Danny Padilla for the Tall, Medium, and Short classes, respectively; Padilla, a remarkable 5'2" athlete from Rochester,
New York, had an excellent shot at a trophy in his class. We
took our team to Pretoria, South Africa—and who greeted us
there but Mike Katz! It seemed that Ben Weider, the very
head of the IFBB, had promised Katz at the last possible second that he could be on the team. That left us with a four-
man team; the United States is permitted to enter only three
athletes. Katz, in an interview, said that Waller should be disqualified; Waller, in an interview, said the same of Katz, and
he swiped Katz's T-shirt for good measure. I, in an interview,
recommended that, because of the sportsmanship each had
shown, both be disqualified. Danny Padilla was finally disqualified, for no real reason that was clear to me except that
someone probably decided that the United States should have
its strongest representation in the heavyweight class. Mike
Katz finished fourth in his class—commendable to be sure,
but worth zero points to the team. Waller won his class and
the overall title. If my original recommendations had been
followed, the team would have done even better.

Of those few who are aware of the contest itself, even
fewer realize the team concept of the U. The reason it means
so much to me is that I want to see an American sweep, all
three classes in one contest. Americans are the world's best

bodybuilders by far, and a sweep seems fitting. But it has never happened, and I don't think that can be the athletes' fault entirely. Even though excellent bodybuilders from other countries have been taking honors at the U, the United States team should be dominating. The American athletes are the best. But either we louse up the teams we send or our leaders don't light a charge under the right prospects to get ready. I'm sorry to say that there are no true comers in bodybuilding whom I can tell you to watch for soon, not even now that the sport is finally rolling and we know that, in one form or another, over 20 million people train with weights. All the big names in bodybuilding have been around for a while. But they'll all be replaced one day, and the field couldn't be more wide open. Arnold publicly estimates that one bodybuilder in 20 enters the sport in the United States with the contest level in mind, an estimate that is inaccurate by no more than a thousandfold. There are perhaps 1,000 competitive body-builders in America today.

The sport needs new talent, but our management has done little to make bodybuilding attractive to our prospects. Contests are poorly run and poorly promoted, losing money for just about every sponsor around except me (my shows have *never* failed to profit handsomely). No one even thought to use professional publicity and promotion specialists for physique contests until 1975, when I ran a professional com-petition the right way for once. I was the first to offer cash prizes—$3,000, $2,000, and $1,000 for that contest. Not much, but far more than bodybuilders were used to; besides, you've got to start someplace.

I'll admit that some of the blame for poorly run shows goes to the bodybuilders themselves. There are more aspects to running a contest well than you'd believe, requiring all kinds of time and energy. Many bodybuilders happen to have both, but what do they do with them? Train, train, train—that's all they want to do. They spend their time getting ready for all those contests that could be so much better with more help. They will give you all the time and heart you could ask for, as long as a barbell comes attached to your request.

The problem with bodybuilding is this: it's so good for

you that just about everybody is literally in it for his health. No one ever looks past training or, for that matter, past his nose.

I, on the other hand, am not opposed at all to making a healthy *living* out of my sport. And I've achieved that the same way I achieved everything else, through a lot of hard work.

I learned the right way to run a physique contest by appearing in so many that were being run the wrong way. Naturally, the same opportunity to learn is available to all competitive bodybuilders, but they're all too busy training.

Besides being a contestant in all the world's best competitions between 1969 and 1976, I had the added advantage of observing shows as a guest poser. This is how the top 10 or 12 bodybuilders make *some* money from the sport. (None is to be had for winning contests. The Olympia, the biggest contest of all, pays the winner only $3,000 or so.) A qualified guest poser, of course, must have won a title more prestigious than the one being offered by the show at which he is a guest. His appearance is designed to increase ticket sales, as you might suppose; but more than that, it's a treat for the crowd, a simple statement that here's the way the sport looks when it's really, really played right.

After a contest where I have guest-posed, I usually make it a point to invite one or two of the best athletes to come to California for a higher order of competition. Whatever other trophies they might have won that evening, their faces show that is the honor they will remember longest.

I was one of the first to drive guest posers' fees into the low four figures as a matter of course. Since I've done that, something curious has happened: the more a guest poser asks these days, the more anxious show promoters seem to have him. I'm a good attraction because I have a loyal following everywhere, and I am always in additional demand because I have my strength exhibitions to offer as well as the posing.

Actually, I've been doing feats of strength since before I was actively bodybuilding—and not just lifting weights, but bending nails and breaking chains. Even today, one of my most common exhibitions is bending steel rods; I wrap the center in a towel and hold the rod in my teeth. It takes about

700 pounds of crushing power to make a ⅝-inch steel bar into a U.

But my most popular stunt by far is blowing up a hot-water bottle like a balloon till it bursts. I use the common rubber variety that comes in any drugstore. (If you want something of a consumer tip, the two-dollar kind is harder for me to burst than the five-dollar kind. I have no idea why.) I require full concentration for this, but I've sneaked a look around now and then between breaths, and I must say that it's probably more fun to watch the people watching me than it is to watch me. From the time the thing is blown up to about the size of my head, they begin scrunching up their faces and flinching in their seats. Actually there's a long way to go; the bag will be nearly the size of my chest before it goes, maybe 20-odd breaths, and the audience will be far more tired than I by then, straining all that time in fear of nothing more than a loud noise, one of the fears we are all born with.

By the way, do *not* try this yourself at home, no matter how strong you think you are. Should you somehow get air in the bag but let go, you're a dead man. The return force of that air will be something on the order of 300 to 500 psi, equivalent pressure, and it will blow away the air sacs in your lungs like so much wet tissue.

I've also used my strength in situations other than as an athlete or as a guest poser. When I was in Munich, it seemed as though fighting were part of not just every night, but of each different beer hall I went into. One guy would swing at a second; he'd swing back but miss and hit a third—and there went the whole place up for grabs, just like in a Hollywood Western. The two guys who started the whole mess would frequently walk out on the fight with their arms around each other, while I'd be left in the middle. But one night Arnold and I emerged from an evening of rare peace in a beer hall, and I had some unused energy and a casual attitude to go with it. There was a mule-drawn cart in the street, and it seemed quite the natural thing to do to unhitch the mule, pick it up on my shoulders, and carry it across the street. So I did.

I had been around farm animals long enough to know how to keep the beast at ease. The mule weighed 500 pounds

The bar.

or so—no problem. I drew some of the strangest looks from passers-by. "I was going to suggest we haul ass, Franco," I heard Arnold call out, "but you're going a little far."

I learned equally spontaneously that I was capable of lifting a car, too. I was in a big hurry one day, and had found a parking place with millimeters to spare. But because I was rushing, I fouled up the parking job three times in a row. Fuming, I stormed out of the car and grabbed the rear bumper, meaning only to skid it into place. But the rear

The hot water bottle.
Courtesy of Benno Dahmen

wheels leaped off the ground as well, and there I was handling a Fiat like a wheelbarrow. "Oh," I said, pleasantly surprised, and I swung the rear half of the vehicle into place.

Two guys were lurching by, and one of them stopped and gaped at me.

"What's the matter with you?" the other asked. "You'll catch flies."

"That—did you see—*that guy lifted his car! He picked up his car!*"

When a jack isn't handy.

His friend looked over at me. I smiled agreeably.

"Sure he did," he said. "I was you, I'd get some good hot coffee in me on the way home."

Another time, after a few beers, I rearranged the cars on my block, alternating the front wheels of one with the rear wheels of another, on and off the curb, till I had this tidy series of Vs all down the block. Being this strong does give you something to do with your time.

But you can't heave an auto around on a contest stage, so I have to choose from among bending rods, exploding a hot-water bottle, or, if the auditorium will permit weights (not all do), some plain dead-lifting, in addition to my posing. I begin the dead-lift exhibition with 405 pounds, three repetitions; then I add weight in 90-pound increments, a 45-pound plate on each end of the bar. By the time the weight goes to

Franco saves.
Courtesy of Art Zeller

585, I'm down to one repetition. They build the bar to 675, and I agonize through one more lift. Then they add some smaller plates. A pretty girl runs up out of the audience to help with some 2½-pound plates I have somehow forgotten to add, and they announce the total weight: 710. And I lift the huge thing to my waist. Not once. *Three* times. And the audience makes a triumphant noise that sounds like "YAHHHHHH!" That bar must seem like a monster, even a barrier, like the four-minute mile or the seven-foot high jump, or every boss they were ever afraid to talk back to, every villain they wanted John Wayne to eliminate for them, every mother-in-law who was surprised at their success. And I master it for them all.

Showmanship? Of course. I am no amateur.

It is guest posing, of course, more so than the competition itself, that has taken me around the world. I've guest posed and held bodybuilding seminars in Australia, Japan, Hawaii, South America, all over Europe, Mexico, South Africa, the United States, and Canada. I think it's a great honor, but I can't deny my interest in the business part of it either. I will not enter into arrangements with contest sponsors I don't know (who are few) or whom I can't check out. Too many athletes get a song-and-dance instead of a check for guest posing. But I'm a practical man, and I always make it my business to get paid promptly and in full. In Guadalajara, my compensation included cash, a trophy, a *sombrero*, and an engraved barrel full of tequila.

A welcome in Belize, British Honduras. *Courtesy of Dr. Anita Columbu*

5

The Winners

I can't work out any more when I go on the road. The word gets out, 200 people show up, and it gets impossible. They pretend to train, but instead they put down the weights, hang around, and stare. I don't mean to be ungracious; it just happens. When you put in the hours and effort to do something in this sport, you can't help respecting someone who has done it all. I always did; I still do.

Other athletes have no problem concentrating on their training in front of audiences, and I'll admit I enjoy watching visiting bodybuilders get to work when they come to California for contests. This is called "blitzing," and it's pretty much akin to cramming for final exams; the contestants usually come to California at least a week before the competition. By then their routines are a compromise between the weight they normally use to attain size and the number of repetitions they do for definition. It's the most weight they can handle for the most times, pure and simple, and their last repetitions will make one wince. When the body is used to 8 or 10 "reps," and then those go to 12 or 15, the last ones really hurt; and contest bodybuilders don't dare cheat the exercise by borrowing from other muscles to jerk the weight around, because that defeats their original purpose.

How the athlete goes about cracking his pain barrier is largely a personal technique. I used to achieve it by thinking about tranquil things: blue sky, green grass, white and fleecy clouds and sheep. I'm pretty sure that men like Mike Katz get there the hardest way, through fury, something to prove with every repetition; the very rhythm of their routines is the tune called for them early on by bullies and oafs. (And Arnold, of

The winners, short class, 1975 Olympia.

course, need only dwell on his wonderfulness.) The proof of this can be seen by a careful viewing of *Pumping Iron;* watch the expressions on our faces as we pose and see who's grinding it out and who's having fun. Katz and other similarly motivated athletes have never beaten me, and that cannot be a coincidence.

I'll admit there is a measure of gloating in my watching athletes sweat out a last-week contest countdown. I never did that. I can understand the desire behind it, but the fact is that there are pretty severe limits to what you can accomplish in one week, especially for a contest-level athlete. I preferred to

The only known effective treatment for "love handles."
Courtesy of Dr. Anita Columbu

take it easy with the weights and run instead. Running is the best trimming exercise that I or anybody else knows of, far better than sit-ups or side bends or any of those exercises. I'm not talking about jogging, which has great cardiovascular benefits but is not nearly as efficient as running for trunk exercise because the knees don't come up as high. Running is how we deal with "love handles," also called "snake bite kits," the universal male fat packs just above the hips. You may see fat people trying to run, but you'll never see a fat runner. One of the world's very best bodybuilders, Robin Robinson of California, is an ex-sprinter. I'm capable of jogging for miles without any problem, but give me a good ten-block dash any time. You get it over and done with—and you know my fondness for conserving time.

What I'd also accomplish, with that precontest layoff, was to make my body extremely receptive to a backstage pump. The muscles would be virtually hungry by then, and I could get pumped easily minutes before appearing, just when I wanted it most.

Upon arriving for the afternoon's pre-judging, bodybuilders who have not seen one another that week will usually greet one another with those by-the-thumb handshakes. After all, they are "soul brothers" of sorts, too. I've also noted that contestants will arrive showing as little as they possibly can of their accomplishments. Loose-fitting jogging suits, baggy jeans, or just modest street clothes are the order of the day. They can't completely hide shoulder and arm size, but that's just the tip of the iceberg. You'll see some form-fitting T-shirts, and short-sleeved shirts rolled way up, but almost always their wearers will be in the audience, not the competition. The contestants do gain something of a psychological edge by concealing their best from their opponents until contest time; but I also think it's significant that the bodybuilders who show off are invariably *not* the ones who compete. That is not the true athlete's attitude.

The contestants will talk about one another, too, and the talk usually runs either to praise for a third party or to a putdown for the speaker. They speak either of size or of how "ripped" somebody is. That means "highly defined" in bodybuilding jargon. At least, I *assume* that's what they're talking about.

"Seen Mike? *Big,* man."

"Yeah. Jeez. Me, I keep getting a little bit better, a little more ripped, but I can't get the size. I just gotta get out here to California if I'm ever gonna bulk up. Like you. Shit." Everybody wants to come to California. California cures everything.

Bodybuilders and true enthusiasts of the sport make up the pre-judging audience. This event is held in the afternoon, takes two to three hours and is generally conducted as though

Pre-judging.

there were no audience present. A moderator will talk the contestants through their poses for the judges' benefit and will address the crowd only incidentally. From the pre-judging, the first three awards in each class are decided, classes being determined by height or weight depending on how the contest is being run. (I divide my contest classes by weight: under 165, 166 to 198, and over 198, the heavyweights.) No one poses individually; you pose with the rest of your class, perhaps later with one or two others in your class. What's left for the evening contest is to determine the first three *overall* winners, regardless of size class, and that is when the athletes perform their individual posing routines.

Naturally, it makes all kinds of sense to have good bodybuilders help out with the show. At my last contest, the Amateur American Championships of the AFAB/IFBB, I had two of the best in the world—Frank Zane and Arnold Schwarzenegger. Frank was my afternoon moderator, an excellent liaison between judges and contestants. Arnold spent some time backstage, advising each class how much time they had left, or talking, if that was what anybody wanted to do. Men like Frank and Arnold know what the athletes are going through mentally, of course, and know how to keep them at ease to do their best.

It's more important to get a good pump for the prejudging than for the finals, as that's when the results are largely determined. Very few auditoriums will permit weights backstage; they scuff floors and chip paint if used carelessly. So that's when bodybuilders go creative. Favorite backstage warmup techniques include wide-grip chinning on coat racks, pushups between two chairs, and straight-arm lateral rises performed with a chair in each hand. It's not the same as one's regular routine, of course, but those improvised warmups get the job done. No muscle is an island, and all those exercises involve muscles secondarily as well as primarily. The chinning gets the juices flowing through the biceps, lats, and all the "cookie cutter" back muscles under the shoulders. The pushups pump the shoulders and chest and help tighten the abdominals; so do the chair raises, which have the added benefit of working the shoulders and trapezius.

My contests always make the judging as simple as it can possibly be; that's fairest to both judges and contestants. I do not want my judges playing around with a complicated points scoring system, because that takes forever and eliminates the judges' valuable instinctive reactions to the physiques they see. If your judges are qualified, and know what to look for, those reactions will almost always be correct, and of course my judges are hand-picked by me and no one else. So I instruct the judges to simply rate each class 1–2–3–4–5–6. Contestants get one point for first, two for second, etc., and when the judges' cards are collected and totaled, the three low scores in each class win, although the results are not announced. It's clean and simple: the best man always wins, and in the least possible time, to boot. I also instruct the judges not to give consideration to symmetry; symmetry is to be *assumed* of my contestants. A bodybuilder with short legs cannot make them longer. I want the contestants judged for muscularity, density,

The backstage pump.

clarity, separation, size, and overall proportion. But I want the symmetry judging left in London.

After I instruct the judges, I try to get a look at the line-up in the locker room. All athletes who enter my events have to send me a picture, but anything is possible in a picture, and you can't even be sure the picture they're sending is truly theirs. So I get downstairs and look for surprises. Most of the time there will be at least one.

One was all I had at my 1977 AFAB/IFBB show. The word was already buzzing around the locker room: "Catch Number Five." This contest is one of the better ones in America; Number Five was every bit of two to three years' hard work away from a novice contest at a local Y. Oh, his chest and shoulders were larger than his waist—give him that. But the highlights of the man's body were clearly his four or five tattoos.

Number Five was a middleweight, the second class to be judged. By the time we were finished judging the lightweights, the word had got out to the few hundred people in the audience. He had a little cult following by the time of his first appearance. You could hear everybody chattering and giggling, "Five! Five! My God, look at Five!"

We divided the middleweight class in half, not in deference to Number Five, but simply because there were 12 entrants in the class and dividing it that way made the judging easier. Number Five would actually not have that bad a time of it in the pre-judging; he would never have the stage to himself, and so the audience could never really center on him as they would if he were to pose solo. I made a note to interview him before the evening show, to see if his attitude merited screaming and striding lessons as well.

Pre-judging lacks the color and drama of the finals, but like so many other sports, it's fascinating if you know *how* to watch. The audiences for pre-judging are comprised pretty much of experts, but I can make the event interesting for first-timers too, even some of those who knock bodybuilding in general. The trick is to put away any previously formed judgments as to what is "gross" or "grotesque," and instead simply try to determine what makes one contestant better than the next. Which ones have visible flaws (calves being an arch villain)? Which are the biggest, and how does their muscle definition compare to that of smaller men? Which poses look graceful and which look awkward (common errors are in not getting the elbows far enough out from the body, and unnecessarily bending the legs or trunk)? Where do you see most clearly what the judges are looking for: muscularity, muscle density, separation, definition, proportion? Give me an open-minded person who is willing to stop shuddering at the very thought of my sport, and I'll bet that person can pick finalists within one or two contests.

It's tense up there. Posing is really a form of isometric exercise, and the athletes can hold any given pose they are asked to strike for only 15 or 20 seconds before the muscles begin to tremble. Watch the lineup as the moderator patiently asks them to make a quarter-turn right; almost without fail, they will all pause a full second, making sure which way right is. Even then, one or two will still turn left and correct themselves with embarrassed grins. There's no penalty for that, but occasionally you'll find a stubborn goat who *won't* turn right because he has a left-side weakness. I don't know what he thinks he's putting over, because merely failing to follow the judges' requests costs him—and points out his weaknesses too.

Watch the contestants shrug their shoulders as one as they anticipate the request for the first rear pose, the lat spread. The most spirited will place the backs of their hands together in front of them, to bring the shoulders up and make the back flare more. It's a very difficult pose to hold, and experienced contestants will usually go into something else— like a double biceps pose—to show complementary muscles and then back to the lat spread again. All this is perfectly above board; the judges may request any pose of any contestant, or group of contestants, at any time. In fact, before the completion of the judging of any class, the moderator will ask the judges if there's anything more they want to see, and of whom.

"Number Five," I could hear Arnold call from his spectator's seat.

"Be nice, Arnold," somebody muttered.

"Don't always have to be nice."

Toward the end of the class judging, the judges will ask two or three athletes to pose, all by number. This can be indicative of results, but is not necessarily so; if you watch very carefully, you can catch a second or less of the strangest expression on the faces of those who weren't called back, an expression they really would rather not show: *"I wonder why they didn't call me?"*

Then the judges will ask the entire class to complete their optional routines. Contestants can still gain favor at this point, but it takes a good sense of rhythm to know when judges are regarding you and when you can catch a couple seconds' relaxation. I saw Arnold trying to help a friend out with hand cues. That's more or less legal, but I don't think it helped that much, because I heard Arnold moan, "Roger works his ass off with nobody looking; when they're judging,

Abdominals. *Courtesy of Caruso*

he goes to sleep." Some less experienced athletes will also lose track of what pose to strike next, and you can see indecision clear from the back rows.

Before the evening finals of my 1977 AFAB/IFBB show, I sought out Number Five. He told me he was a bellhop in a Los Angeles hotel, that he worked out three times a week at a Y, and that he had been training for 13 of his 29 years. Number Five was simple but pleasant, desperately happy to have someone to talk to. No screaming lessons needed here.

I asked to see his optional posing routine. He didn't pose any better than he looked; on the other hand, he didn't do

anything to make himself look worse either. His posing was natural and unaffected; the routine seemed to suit him, but there were no muscles to leap to life, only tattoos.

"How do you feel about posing tonight?" I asked.

"A little nervous," he said. "I guess I'm not in that great shape for this big a contest."

"Have you ever competed before?"

"No."

"Tell me this," I said. "Didn't you think about starting out with a contest where the competition wouldn't be quite so tough?"

MR. OLYMPIA 1974

The posedown, Mr. Olympia, 1974. Four of the all-time greats, left to right: Columbu, Zane, Ferrigno, Schwarzenegger.

Courtesy of Albert Busek

Courtesy of Art Zeller

"Well, it was just an idea," he said. "I wanted to be in a contest, and yours was the first one I heard about, so I entered."

"Have you ever *seen* a contest before?"

"Yes, I saw the Mr. California contest," came the innocent answer, naming an event that featured many of the same athletes mine did. "I should have started with that one."

I decided to let him pose. His natural manner would probably not offend anybody, and his build would provide two minutes' relief for the crowd. Bodybuilding audiences benefit from that. Audiences often tense right along with the posers, and they can get pretty whipped themselves by the time a show ends. If you have ever been in a car being driven too fast for your tastes, and you tried to apply the brakes right where you were sitting, you know what I mean.

"Well," I said, "We'll see you tonight. I suppose the worst that can happen is that you won't win."

"Oh, I'm prepared for *that*," he said. "It was just an idea."

Bodybuilding promoters consistently forget that an audience for competition finals should be "pumped" for the event too, just as the athletes are. A good, responsive audience is a must for the bodybuilders to do their absolute best. So when a contest is run by somebody who knows what he's doing, it will begin not with competition but with something else that can get the audience up quickly. I like to begin my shows with a guest poser, if I can find one good enough, and finish off by guest posing myself while the results are being totaled.

That evening in 1977 I opened my show with one of the best, Mike Mencer of Maryland, 5'9", 220+, the current Mr. America, and an almost certain Universe winner in the next few years. Backstage, there was less activity than you might expect. The important judging, remember, is already done; as the results have not been announced to be sure that everybody tries his hardest that night, the athletes usually sit around assuming the worst, sighing and checking the clock and saying, "Shit."

"Shit. Can't we have *any* iron back here?"

"What for? You look pumped already."

"Yeah, I *wish*. Shit."

Even as proud as they are, contest bodybuilders have been building one another up for so long that they now seem to expect the next man to win. That makes for some peculiar tensions. Just before a Mr. World contest once, I was approached by a Belgian whom I won't embarrass by name although he deserves it.

"Franco," he said, "I know I can't beat you, but I'd like to at least win my class. Is there anything extra I can do before I go on?"

The question infuriated me. I was feeling my oats, no doubt about it; I expected to win the contest (and did), and as the Mr. World representative for another year, I wanted no negative talk on contest premises, not in a sport where Desire is the horse you ride in on.

"For God's sake," I spat out, "what kind of talk is this, 'I can't win'? Who is it that's going to beat you?"

"————."

"Well, here's what I think you should do. Do you have a dumbbell in your training bag?"

"Yes," he said eagerly, anticipating exercise.

"Well, go drop it on ————'s foot. Then you won't have him to beat."

"Huh," the loser said, and walked away. Minutes later, my ears told me that my sarcastic advice had unfortunately been followed to the letter. ———— hobbled out onstage gamely, though, and the judges accepted his excuse. He won his class in spite of his injury.

Mike Mencer got my audience whooping and hollering good and early, as I expected. The show was going beautifully. Solo posing is still done by class, and the lightweights put on a tremendous show. (Lightweights and middleweights may not produce as spectacular a champion as the heavyweights, but almost always, those two classes will give you a better overall competition within their class than the heavies will, and I'm not just being partial.)

Solo posing is done to music. The theme from *Exodus* is traditional now; Wagner is excellent too, as is anything noble. There are several reasons besides showmanship for the music:

Posing
—the 1975 Mr. Olympia.

it helps the bodybuilder find his rhythm during and between poses, and it makes it harder for him to tell what the precise audience reaction to him is. This second reason is important, because without music, he would know within one or two poses if the crowd had already seen his equal or better. So the music must be continuous, to avoid awkward periods of silence while athletes are onstage. When a bodybuilding audience gets good and revved up, they can outdo the music with no problem. But those responses are limited, no more than two or three a show, and I would rather have my contestants concentrating on themselves, not the audience.

Even when a bodybuilder does not receive an overpowering reaction to his first few poses, he can still win the audience over. Bodybuilding crowds spark to anything they haven't already seen, either in other contestants or in that athlete himself. An attractive new pose always refreshes the audience. So will a particularly well-developed muscle group, even if disproportionate to the rest (as an example, only rarely will a contest winner have the very best arms in the field). Good calves and abdominals are other notable crowd-pleasers. And of course, the reason everybody closes with the "Most Muscular," or "Crab," pose is that not only does it contract all the major muscle groups at once, but it also pops ridges, veins, and striations that could not be seen before.

The music ends when the athlete's routine does, of course, and each contestant in turn is introduced with his name, a brief biography, and his contest number. I heard this polite little gasp all around me when Number Five was called, and I looked around and saw fans from the afternoon's prejudging squirming down low into their seats.

For posing music, Number Five drew *Die Walküre,* which was probably just as well; it masked the most peculiar kind of audience sound, a kind of mass "What the hell is *this?*" I am well known to California bodybuilding followers, naturally, and I heard my name being spoken all over, as though Number Five were some sort of personal grand scheme of mine. Onstage, he strained mightily and, here and there, did introduce a new contour or two to his tattoos.

Isn't there a bad dream most of us have about being caught naked in public? This was pretty damn close, but I must say that Number Five seemed unaffected by it all. After their initial 10 or 15 seconds of pure shock, the audience began to cheer him. It was pretty much the sound you hear for an outfielder who finally catches a fly ball after dropping three, but Number Five wouldn't be able to tell that. He finally heard Frank Zane and other purists giggling in the first few rows, and he began to laugh himself. Number Five left the posing platform with a bigger grin and wave for the crowd than the eventual winner did. We sent him a medal afterwards for "Best Effort."

As for me, I took the stage for a strength exhibition after the lightweights, and for dead-lifting after the middles. I saved my own posing till after the heavyweight class. It's easy to look good when you are the only one bending steel rods or dead-lifting mammoth barbells; but when you come out to do what everyone else has been doing all night, that is another kind of challenge. I'm presently two good months away from contest shape; still, for sheer muscle density, I am unequaled in bodybuilding today, and perhaps in bodybuilding ever. My muscles are built to last, with or without daily training, and I draw a special kind of cheer when I show an audience the kind of back real power can mold. Lower back development is a weakness even among champion bodybuilders; but the erector muscles in the lumbar region of my back wind toward a crevice over my spine like twin edges of spiral seashells. Up top, it takes me a series of three contractions to get the lats fully flared. "Jeez," I once heard a guy say, "he could *fly* with that."

The last treat I have for my audiences is to introduce the celebrities who are sitting among them. The sport, or at least the training, has been fashionable in Hollywood for years. Probably the most accomplished actor/bodybuilder is William Smith, of television's *Rich Man, Poor Man,* who is so impressive that his training routines have been reprinted in Weider magazines. I have several actor friends with whom I train when their schedules permit; one of them, John Saxon, was in the audience that night. So were Burt Reynolds, who gained more fame in a single pose than all the athletes in my sport combined after half a century of trying, and Dom DeLuise, who was only

Dead-lifting.
Courtesy of Art Zeller

a few points short of catching up to Number Five.

Then we present the awards, and that's it. My contests award trophies for the first three places in each class, and the first three places overall, nothing more. Everyone goes home early and happy. Other shows keep their audiences bleary-eyed by handing out awards for Best Body Parts till the crack of dawn, but that is total lunacy to me. Do tennis tournaments honor the Best Backhand? Should we wake boxers up off the canvas and fete them for Best Left?

Bodybuilding, like the men who take part in it, is largely

just something you aren't used to seeing. Like any other great sport, it runs a gamut of emotion, beauty, and art—all that you will allow yourself to see. Approach the sport with an open mind, and it will fill that mind with pictures of athletes and spirit and competition, just like the game of your choice.

It wasn't till I got married that I attained my absolute peaks in both strength and physique, and I'm not merely singing the praises of love, as formidable as those powers are. Divorce rates are sadly high among competitive bodybuilders. When a man spends hours and hours in a gym, hours more in the sun, and hours more than *that* practicing posing, he either appears to be or genuinely is engrossed with himself, and any kind of comfortable relationship with him requires a very understanding woman.

In that respect, I'd rate myself the luckiest bodybuilder of all time. Not only is Anita a superb doctor of chiropractic, with a vast knowledge of body mechanics, but she understands the philosophy and science of bodybuilding, too. The frequent chiropractic adjustments she gives me are an invaluable part of my training, and as we are both doctors of chiropractic now, we constantly research new and improved training methods together. We're both experts on nutrition, too, and she prepares only the best natural foods for us.

With insights into the human anatomy that complemented mine perfectly, Anita was instrumental in my beginning, pursuing, and completing chiropractic college. Remember, I began that grueling six-year course with a background of one year's English. As proud as I am of my accomplishments, I don't at all mind saying that I couldn't have done those things alone.

For all Anita's encouragement and help, she has had the time to see me compete only once, in the 1976 Olympia, the finest contest of my life.

That year represented my fourth try at the contest between the best of the best; in the three previous years, I had won my class but lost the overall to Arnold. Winning contests was not critical to me then. I was already well established at

The doctors Columbu.

An adjustment from Anita.

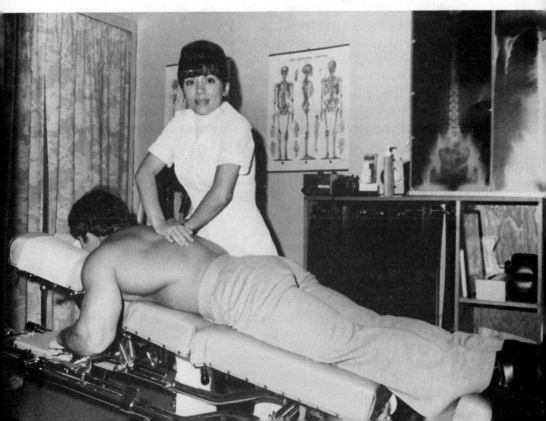

the top of the sport; what I basically wanted to do was give my following a good show, which I did.

And the thrill of competing in the Olympia itself carried me a long way. After all, it was my "Title Fight at the Garden" from a decade before (the 1974 Olympia was held in the Garden's Felt Forum). You cannot enter the Olympia unless you have already won a Universe or a Mr. World, and thus been acclaimed one of the world's very best long before the judges begin adding their totals. Only three men in history had ever won an Olympia before me. Even the guy who finishes last in an O looks phenomenal. All the contestants are super athletes who have added some showmanship to their builds and posing; and Olympia audiences, the most knowledgeable and enthusiastic in the sport, respond to that. Those cheers—there's a magic that always attends seeing the Best of anything, very similar to the magic that goes with the First of anything, and you can hear it in the cheers. It's a sound that seems to come from under the belly button someplace; it makes you think of white heat, and it's so strong and pure you can sense yourself riding its crest. It doesn't matter how old the audience is, or how big it is, or even whom they've come to see. I've heard that sound for Julius Erving, and for Mick Jagger, too, and I can tell you it's exactly the same.

But I made up my mind that I did want it all in 1976. Merely putting on a good show in the O would not do; I had decided that I would be unbeatable. I had been acting out the fable of "The Ant and the Grasshopper" with my bodybuilding friends for six years by then, poring over books in chiropractic college and at home while they trained and sunned. They wanted to grow as bodybuilders; I wanted to grow as a human being. The story was nearly over (I successfully took my four-day, 2,100-question Board Exams just four days before the contest), and I wanted the happiest ending that could be written.

My first decision concerning the 1976 Olympia was a maverick one: I would train at home. Among competitive bodybuilders, it's almost axiomatic that you must have the atmosphere of a gym to do your best. But once again, my initial goal was to conserve time. I estimated that time traveling to and from the gym, and in the locker room, was costing me an hour and a half daily, 'way more than I could afford. So I constructed my own gym in my garage, buying four tons of weight and designing other special equipment I would need to train alone. I caught monumental flak from the gym and beach crowds; the notion of training alone at home was enough to move everybody to write me off for the contest. But you don't win contests, or hardly anything else in life, by merely listening to what others think. I had work to do.

My only appearances at the gym were every two or three weeks, to check the progress of others, and I always left happy because I was clearly showing everybody my heels. Art Zeller would come over now and then to report on the field, too, and his was an opinion I really respected because of Art's skill, as the world's best physique photographer, in looking for both strong and weak points.

But mostly I stayed out of sight, as though working on a secret invention. Six months' trial-and-error experimentation had finally yielded the optimum arm routine for me, for one thing; six months of picking and choosing, this before that, but not before *that*. Work two weeks; observe; throw that out; try another version. The arms are more complicated to train than you'd think because they are composed of smaller muscles. When a bodybuilder achieves maximum arm bulk— actually a very common error—he sacrifices definition and density; thus the arm may really look smaller than it could.

But arms are just one detail. The fresh point of view that came with training alone at home had enhanced my overall muscularity and definition. You can't believe the difference attitude alone makes.

I was not satisfied with the edge in physique that I knew I had on the field to begin with. Rumors were circulating, rumors that indicated that politics definitely favored other contestants. I had not come this far to reenact my adventures with Tampellini in Verona, or with the two Universe contests in Europe. I would have to build the kind of victory margin that would leave no possible way for anyone else to win. So I did.

I left for Columbus, Ohio, at 190 pounds of pure muscle, the most I ever weighed. The auditorium was packed for the afternoon pre-judging, and that is certainly unique in our

At the peak—Mr. Olympia, 1976. *Courtesy of Art Zeller*

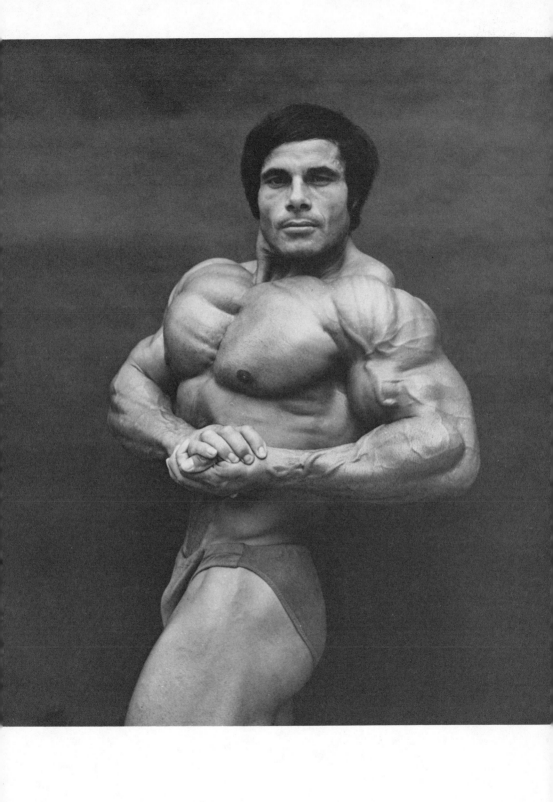

The curl.

sport. The whopping crowd began making that wonderful sound as soon as we walked onstage, and it occurred to me, *"Here it is, all set for you, just the way you saw it all years ago. This time, you better make it perfect."*

Both the pre-judging and the evening performance seemed endless to me, and I've never been good at waiting. I told myself some awful stories about judging mischief, but my two Mr. Universe fiascos in Europe had conditioned me to do that. The results of the eight o'clock evening performance were not announced till after midnight. But when they were, I remember having enough strength left for a victory leap; at 5'5", I think I could have damn near dunked a basketball with that one. Then I went to find my wife and share a good, happy cry.

No bodybuilder in history under 200 pounds can match my record (three times Mr. World, three U's, and an O); no one else has ever achieved both strength and physique laurels so often. But the accomplishment that makes me proudest is that I was the first bodybuilder ever in that size class to win both the *overall* Universe and Olympia titles. You don't have to be the biggest to win. You just have to want it the most.

I caught this punk stealing my gym bag once. I was finished training and was about to enter my car when I remembered something I had left in the gym. So I left my bag on the hood while I went back inside, and, Southern California being what it is, there went my gym bag. It was just pungent shorts, tanktop, shoes, and the like, but that wasn't the point. The kid had covered the length of the parking lot by the time I saw him.

"You can stop there if you know what's good for you," I called out. "If I have to come after you, I'll run over your *head!*" The words froze him in his tracks.

"Now come here to me." He obeyed as though in a trance. I grabbed his shirt front in one hand, lifted him off the ground, and sat him down on my car. I slapped him once, not hard; fear would hurt him far worse than I wanted to myself. "You will *never* do this again!" I hissed. Then I lifted him up again and carried him into the gym.

"Arnold! Come here!"

Arnold came over. He was at about 240 pounds then, good and pumped, as big as he ever was.

"I caught this man stealing my training bag. Now, do you have something to say to him?"

There was a good crowd in the gym that day. Some of the world's biggest bodies began edging up behind Arnold. Up front, Arnold glowered skillfully—acting is not all that new to him.

"You do this again, you die," Arnold finally growled. My thief seemed to have aged 30 years or so. Arnold's chorus muttered menacing things too, as I picked the kid up for the last time and hauled him outside. When I put him down, he took one backward step and froze.

"Well?" I said.

Arnold had followed us outside. "Like a fish," he said. "I don't think he knows he is free."

Maybe he was in shock, at that. I remembered my own thoughts about what was real and what was not, the unreality of there even *being* a California in the first place, and of the capabilities of American-trained muscles, and all the other day/night differences between two worlds. I had just transported this kid, too, into a world of villains of supernatural size and power, a secret and sweaty master race. I hadn't believed it, either, the first time I entered it, even though I was far closer to it than he could ever be. The gym shoes and shorts of America would be safe from that thief for some time to come.

"It's all right," I said. "You can go."

I don't mean to sound traitorous, but there are really more important things to do than win physique contests. When I came to America seven years ago, I saw a lot of huge guys training hard, and most of them were broke. Today they're still looking good, training, and broke; and I have won all the titles they were training for, even the biggest, and have earned an excellent living with a capacity for more as well. It's a matter of priorities.

In bodybuilding, there is truly nothing beyond the Olympia. I could choose to defend my title as Arnold did, but what for—an asterisk in a record book that almost no one reads?

I plan to stay active in promoting my sport as long as time permits. But I expect to be deeply involved as a Doctor of Chiropractic very soon. Either way, I'll be active in showing people how good the body can truly feel, repaying a sport that has sent me around the world and let me spend a good part of my life doing what I do best and enjoy most.

I was able to combine chiropractic college with training because of several factors. For one thing, I had long since learned to compress my workouts to 90 minutes or two hours. I was gladly willing to sacrifice the time other athletes take for four- to six-hour routines, sunbathing, and the like. My studies limited the time I had for my part in *Pumping Iron,* too. But you've simply got to put first things first.

It's hard to imagine a more ideal discipline to combine with bodybuilding than the study of chiropractic. I spent seven hours a day for six years learning the body by *theory,* plus another two hours or slightly less daily in the *practical* application of what I had learned. My studies unquestionably made me a greater bodybuilder; my bodybuilding made me a better Doctor of Chiropractic. (So did the fact that I fell in love with and married a brilliant Doctor of Chiropractic.) One chiropractic technique alone, called "muscle balancing," helps the muscles perform up to 15 percent better.

What will happen to the muscles when I can't train any more? That's the question asked more often than any other of bodybuilders, and the answer is the exact opposite of the myth. The muscles will not turn to fat; that is impossible, as muscles are composed of muscle cells, and fat of fat cells, and one does not turn into the other any more than apples become oranges. Acutally, what will happen is that I'll systematically *lose* weight with a curtailed diet. When I was blitzing, my average daily intake was 10,000 calories, spread over four or five well-spaced and balanced meals, dinner being the lightest because it's the one you burn up least. But my everyday diet is less spectacular; three good meals of all natural foods, high-protein–low-carbohydrate, lots of meat and fish, nothing processed, no sugar or fats or white flour—all just as on Sardinia where I began. Both my chiropractic studies and my bodybuilding training have made me an expert on nutrition as well as the anatomy, and I expect to be healthy, muscular, and strong all my days.

Filming *Pumping Iron*. *Courtesy of Art Zeller*

Filming "The Streets of San Francisco."

Steve Reeves is an excellent example of how far the sport of bodybuilding has come. He won his Universe about 25 years ago, and at that time he was thought to be one of the very best ever. But the fact is, Reeves looked far better in those silly films than he ever did in contests; and at his very *best,* he'd have trouble competing at the statewide level today. The best of the best in bodybuilding today, I think, stand up to Bob Beamon and Dwight Stones and the handful of other champion athletes who have demonstrated how little we know of man's real potential with his body.

I'll tell you one thing, though. Football players block and tackle other football players, basketball players guard other basketball players, and so on. But each bodybuilder takes on Nature and himself, respectively the most potent force and the most formidable opponent on earth, and he wins over both. The time bodybuilders spend in gyms seems awesome to some, but they are really getting to know themselves better, and to like themselves better in the bargain. In light of that, the time bodybuilders put into their sport is certainly minor compared to what they take out.

Bodybuilding's winners are obvious long before any trophies are handed out. Every last one is my idea of a winner, even that incredible Number Five. Whatever it is you do in life, you can never grow in self-esteem unless you get good and pumped first and stay that way. And time you spend without a pump is time you can never get back again. I wouldn't let any opportunities get away if I were you. I never did.

The end.

BE SURE TO READ FRANCO COLUMBU'S OTHER GREAT BOOKS—AND DON'T FORGET THE FRANCO COLUMBU POSTER

23¼" × 35"
COLOR